THE BYE BITCH BOOK

How to Leave What Breaks You, Choose What Heals You, and Stop Entertaining What God, Therapy, and Your Sanity Never Approved

By L.A. Walker

SPEAKING IN VOLUMES
A MULTIMEDIA PUBLISHING COMPANY

Published by **Speaking in Volumes**
Imprint: **Big Sis**

ISBN: **978-1-956070-14-9**

For more information:
wwwbigsis.life

Printed in the United States of America.

TABLE OF CONTENTS

- Dedication
- Preface
- Why This Book is Called
- A Note Before We Begin

SEGMENT I — STORIES
Where it happened.

SEGMENT II — DISRUPTING THE PATTERN
Turning Trauma Into Power
What happened?

SEGMENT III — CAN WE CHAT...
How did it happen?

- Big Sis' Final Word — Before You Rise
- Speaking In Volumes

DEDICATION

To every woman who stayed too long, loved too hard, forgave too quickly,

and abandoned herself too silently.

To the ones who thought heartbreak would break them but still rose the next morning.

To the ones rebuilding their peace one boundary at a time.

To the women who finally whispered the most powerful prayer:

"Choose me."

This book is for you.

PREFACE

Every woman carries stories she survived, outgrew, endured, or learned too late.

This book was created to honor those stories and to speak to the woman standing at the edge of her next becoming.

We wrote The Bye Bitch Book for the moments when courage whispers louder than fear, when endings become sacred, and when choosing yourself becomes the most spiritual act of all.

Within these pages lives humor, heartbreak, insight, and the unmistakable voice of Big Sis—a guide who speaks truth without hesitation and hope without restraint.

May this book remind you that release is not failure, boundaries are not cruelty, and walking away is sometimes the highest form of self-respect.

To every woman reclaiming her voice, her worth, and her peace—this book is yours.

L.A. Walker

Why This Book Is Called

The Bye Bitch Book

This title is not about cruelty.
It's about clarity.

"Bye, bitch" is not an insult here.
It's a boundary.

It's what a woman finally says—not out loud, but internally—when she realizes she has outgrown what has been draining her, shrinking her, or quietly breaking her spirit.

It's the moment she stops negotiating with pain.
The moment she stops explaining herself to people who benefit from her confusion.
The moment she chooses peace over performance.

This book is not encouraging anger.
It is encouraging **release**.

Sometimes "bye" is said to a relationship.
Sometimes it's said to a pattern.
Sometimes it's said to a version of yourself that survived—but no longer serves you.

And sometimes, the most loving thing you can do is walk away without a speech, without a scene, and without burning yourself down in the process.

This is not a breakup manual.
It's a **self-return**.

So if the title makes you laugh, flinch, or feel seen—you're in the right place.

Because this book isn't about leaving recklessly.
It's about leaving **intact**.

Welcome.

Acknowledgments

Melani Sanders (@justbeingmelani)

We don't ever recall anyone rising as quickly and quietly as you while showing so much grace.
Your selfless sharing of encouragement to those of us who dare to dream is unmatched.
You are a blessing to many. Your words have inspired us to remain faithful to our dreams.

Thank you.

To the Women Whose Love Carries Me
Your strength, wisdom, humor, and prayers shape the pages of this book.

Thank you for showing up for me— and for yourselves — in ways that matter.

Toshia Marvin	Jennifer Wampler	Josephine O'Brien
Nikki Murdock	Debbie Hall	Olga Rios
Kelly Smith	Deborah Lanz	Angie Pohlman
Winnie Schulman	Marty Pereida	Nicole Williams
Linda Simpson	Cassandra Sanders	Gloria Jones
Judi Di Gioia	Skye Dee Miles	Cendrene Neil
Sarah O'Connell	Felecia Neal Lee	Yvette Williams

Dr. Marcia Norris

You are the circle I return to.
You are the voice I hear when my strength feels thin.
You are the evidence that women standing together can survive anything
—

and create everything.

This book bows to you.

Author Bio

L.A. Walker is the creator of Big Sis—a grounded, lived voice centered on clarity, emotional honesty, and choosing yourself without shame.

Through storytelling, reflection, and direct truth-telling, her work explores relationship dynamics, emotional disorientation, and the moments when self-trust begins to return. She writes for people who knew something was wrong long before they could explain why—and who are now ready to name what actually happened.

Walker is also the founder of Life Be Lifing, a platform dedicated to personal clarity, creative expression, and emotional self-rescue. Her work prioritizes recognition over diagnosis and understanding over blame.

She lives in the space between compassion and truth—and believes both can exist at the same time.

Website: www.lifebelifing.shop

Big Sis reflections: www.bigsis.life

Who Big Sis Is — And Why She's Here

Big Sis is not a character.
She is a voice many women already know.

She's the friend who tells the truth without cruelty.
The one who can laugh with you and still hold you accountable.
The woman who's lived long enough to recognize patterns—and bold enough to name them.

Big Sis exists because too many women are taught how to endure, but not how to exit.
How to explain pain, but not how to interrupt it.
How to survive relationships, but not how to leave the ones that quietly dismantle them.

Big Sis doesn't diagnose.
She doesn't rescue.
She doesn't position herself as the authority over your life.

Her role is simpler—and harder.

She reflects back what you already know but haven't trusted yet.
She names what you've been minimizing.
She reminds you where your power lives when you've forgotten how to access it.

Big Sis doesn't give permission.
She doesn't hand out instructions for living.
She doesn't replace your intuition.

She helps you recognize it again.

This voice exists because clarity is often more healing than comfort, and truth—delivered with care—can be the difference between staying stuck and choosing yourself.

Big Sis is not the power source.
She simply points to where yours already is.

How To Use This Book

This book is not meant to be read like a novel.
And it's not meant to be studied like a manual.

These stories are mirrors.

Each one reflects a moment, a dynamic, or a pattern that many people recognize but rarely slow down long enough to examine. You are not meant to agree with every story—or see yourself in all of them.

You are meant to notice what *moves* you.

Read one story at a time.
Pause when something stings, irritates, or feels uncomfortably familiar.
That reaction is information.

Ask yourself:

- What part of this story feels known to me?
- Where have I seen this pattern before?
- What did I excuse, minimize, or misunderstand?
- How did this situation make me feel then—and how do I feel about it now?

You are not required to judge yourself for what you tolerated.
You are not required to defend anyone else's behavior.
You are only asked to be honest.

This book works best when you let it slow you down—not rush you to conclusions. Clarity comes from observation, not pressure.

If a story doesn't apply, let it pass.
If one lingers, sit with it.

The purpose of these pages is not to relive pain—but to understand it well enough that you don't repeat it.

Read with curiosity.
Respond with honesty.
And take what helps you choose differently moving forward.

A NOTE BEFORE WE BEGIN

This book is written in conversation with women.

It speaks directly to the emotional labor, relationship dynamics, expectations, and lived experiences that women are most often asked to carry—quietly, repeatedly, and without acknowledgment.

That said, men are welcome here.

If you are a man reading this book, you are invited—not to feel accused, corrected, or put on trial—but to observe, reflect, and take what applies to your own growth. Many men read these pages to better understand their partners, sisters, daughters, friends, colleagues, and themselves. Some read it to learn how conversations feel on the receiving end. Some read it simply to listen.

This book is not anti-men.

It is pro-clarity, pro-accountability, and pro-emotional literacy.

Women, historically and socially, have been expected to process pain out loud, in community, often while still performing strength. Men, just as often, are taught to process pain inwardly, privately, or through action rather than language. Neither approach makes pain disappear—it simply changes how it shows up.

So if parts of this book don't feel "tailored" to you, that's intentional.

Listening is also participation.

Read with curiosity, not defensiveness.

Take what helps.

Leave what doesn't.

And if something stings—pause there.

Growth usually does.

Welcome to the conversation.

SEGMENT I
STORIES
Where it happened

The Road Trip That Changed My Life

SECTION 1

Five and a half hours on the road.
A four-year-old in the backseat.
And a heart full of anticipation I didn't yet know was fragile.

My partner had asked me to pick up her daughter from school and bring her with me to Cleveland. I was excited. It was the first time we'd been apart for a full week. I imagined a reunion. Relief. Something warm is waiting on the other side of the drive.

Traffic was brutal. Escaping it felt like victory.
Pulling into the driveway felt like an arrival.

But instead of a welcome, I got this:

"Let's go to the liquor store."

Back in the car.

Ohio shuts down liquor sales on Sundays, so everyone floods the stores on Saturday. Practical, I told myself. Normal. I ignored the disappointment. I ignored the feeling.

Then I noticed something else.

My partner got into the front seat—next to the driver.

We hadn't seen each other in a week.
And suddenly there was distance where closeness should have been.

I ignored that too.

She and our friend's sister went into the store. They encouraged me to stay in the car and rest. No argument from me. I was exhausted. Five and a half hours of conversation with a four-year-old had taken more out of me than I realized.

They came back.

The car didn't move.

And then my partner turned around, looked directly at me, and said words that sounded like they belonged in a psychological thriller:

"I'm going home with you… and getting myself prepared to move back here to be with her."

I remember thinking—*Did she just say that to me?*

From that moment on, everything blurred.

The time stuck in Cleveland with the lovebirds.
The long drive back to Chicago.
The weeks that followed.
The day I drove her to the airport and waved goodbye.

This almost killed me.

And if Uncle Sam hadn't accepted me into the Army, I honestly don't know if I would have survived it.

COMMENTARY

This is the moment betrayal stops being emotional and becomes disorienting.

Not loud.
Not dramatic.
Just a sudden collapse of meaning.

This is where the body realizes something before the mind can catch up. Where shock disguises itself as compliance. Where survival kicks in quietly.

Nothing prepares you for being *used* as transportation into your own abandonment.

SECTION 2

I didn't scream.
I didn't argue.
I didn't demand answers.

I did what so many people do when reality breaks too fast—I went numb.

I stayed.
I endured.
I carried on through shared spaces that felt contaminated with truth I hadn't consented to know yet.

I told myself I would process it later.

Later came slowly.
And painfully.

COMMENTARY

This is where people confuse strength with silence.

Shock often looks like calm.
Compliance often looks like grace.
And staying doesn't always mean agreement—it often means the nervous system hasn't caught up yet.

SECTION 3

Eventually, I left.

Not triumphantly.
Not confidently.

Just intact enough to keep moving.

I drove her to the airport.
I waved.
I watched her disappear.

And something in me broke open instead of apart.

COMMENTARY

Sometimes survival doesn't look like empowerment.

It looks like an escape.

And sometimes the thing that saves you isn't closure—it's structure. Routine. Purpose. Something bigger than the moment that almost ended you.

SECTION 4

The Army didn't heal me.

But it kept me alive long enough to heal myself.

Distance gave me perspective.
Discipline gave me grounding.
And time gave me language for what had happened.

COMMENTARY

This is the quiet truth no one says out loud:

You don't always leave because you're ready.
Sometimes you leave because staying would cost you your life.

How Would You Have Handled This?

(Big Sis Manhattan Edition)

☐ **A.**
Lost your composure publicly
and spent years replaying it privately.

☐ **B.**
Stayed polite, stayed silent,
and processed the damage later.

☐ **C.**
Demanded answers from someone
already packing their future.

☐ **D.**
Left without confrontation
because survival outranks explanations.

☐ **E.**
Did whatever kept you breathing
until you could stand again.

Big Sis Reality Check

If someone can rewrite your life in one sentence,
The priority isn't understanding them.

It's getting yourself somewhere safe enough
to recover from the shock.

And for the record—
you don't owe dignity to someone who just took your oxygen.

Nothing tests your character like being handed a life plot twist without consent.

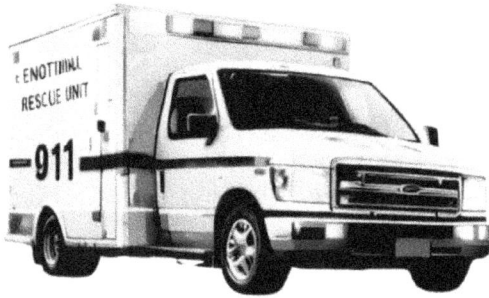

Big Sis Says

YOU WEREN'T STUPID –
YOU WERE HOPEFUL.
NOW YOU'RE HEALING,
YOU'RE WISER,
AND
YOU'RE UNAVAILABLE
FOR NONSENSE.

Falling in Love With Someone Else's Someone

Love at First Bite · Tears in a To-Go Cup

SECTION 1

It never starts as an affair.
It starts as a connection.

Cecilia met Margo the way people always do—unexpectedly. A conversation that lasted longer than planned. Laughter that felt familiar too quickly. The kind of spark that makes you forget context.

They talked over food.
Then coffee.
Then "just one more minute."

Gay, straight, they, them—his or hers—it never matters.
The script is always the same.

Someone casually mentions a partner. Almost apologetically. As if it's a footnote, not a headline.

It's complicated.
We're not happy.
I don't feel seen.

And somehow, instead of stopping the moment, it deepens it.

Because now it feels special.
Chosen.
Secret.

Love at first bite.

COMMENTARY

This is where people confuse chemistry with destiny.

Connection feels rare when it arrives unexpectedly. And when someone is already emotionally starving, even crumbs feel like a feast.

This isn't about morality yet.
It's about momentum.

SECTION 2

The relationship grows in margins.

Texts between obligations.
Calls that end too quickly.
Plans that never quite materialize.

Cecilia tells herself she's not asking for much.
Margo tells herself she'll make a decision soon.

They share intimacy without infrastructure.
Emotion without commitment.
Hope without protection.

And every promise lives in the future.

Soon.
When things settle.
After this phase.

COMMENTARY

This is where people mistake patience for virtue.

Waiting feels noble when you believe you're waiting for love. But there's a difference between timing and avoidance.

One person is suspended.
The other remains anchored somewhere else.

SECTION 3

Eventually, reality interrupts.

The partner doesn't leave.
The situation doesn't change.
The future keeps being postponed.

And the relationship ends the same way it began—quietly.

No dramatic goodbye.
No villain speech.
Just distance.

Cecilia cries alone in her car.
Coffee cup shaking in her hand.
Tears caught in a to-go lid that was never meant to hold this much.

Love at first bite.
Grief to go.

COMMENTARY

This is the part no one romanticizes.

Being chosen privately but denied publicly erodes self-trust. You start questioning your worth—not because you weren't enough, but because you were never available to be chosen fully.

SECTION 4

Later, Cecilia understands something she couldn't see then:

People who are already committed don't fall in love accidentally.
They fall in love *selectively*.

They take what they need without dismantling what they already have.

And the person on the outside pays the cost.

COMMENTARY

This dynamic hurts because it offers intimacy without safety.

It teaches you to accept partial presence.
To negotiate your needs down.
To confuse secrecy with devotion.

But here's the truth:

If someone belongs to someone else, they cannot belong to you—no matter how real it feels.

How Would You Have Handled This?

☐ **A.**
Stayed because the connection felt rare
and hoped it would outrun reality.

☐ **B.**
Accepted emotional intimacy
without structural commitment.

☐ **C.**
Waited patiently
while your life stayed on pause.

☐ **D.**
Walked away early
even though it hurt more up front.

☐ **E.**
Recognized that love without availability
is just longing with good lighting.

Big Sis Reality Check

If someone's life doesn't have room for you,
their feelings don't change that.

Love that has to hide
eventually disappears.

And it almost always leaves the same souvenir—
tears in a to-go cup.

If they were really leaving for you, you wouldn't be ordering
comfort drinks alone.

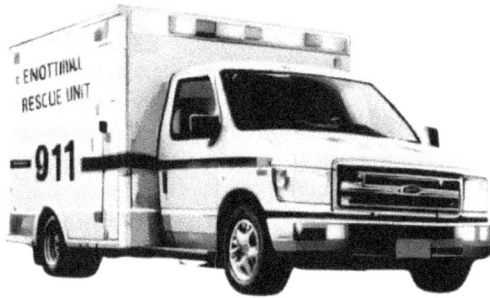

Big Sis Says

STOP CALLING IT A "MISUNDERSTANDING". YOU UNDERSTOOD IT – YOU JUST DIDN'T WANT TO BELIEVE IT.

Alfreda And Charli

The Fight That Came Out of Nowhere

SECTION 1

Alfreda and Charli had been together for four years.

They were compatible in every way that mattered. Same values. Same humor. Same rhythm. Friends admired how easily they moved together through life.

Most days felt calm. Connected. Good.

That's what made the fights so confusing.

They didn't build.
They detonated.

Everything could be fine—laughing in the kitchen, sharing a story, relaxed—and then, without warning, Alfreda would turn.

"You're disrespecting me."
"I don't like the way you're talking to me."

Charli would freeze.

Nothing had changed. No raised voice. No insult. No provocation. And yet suddenly she was standing in the middle of an argument she didn't recognize, defending herself against something that didn't exist five minutes earlier.

COMMENTARY

This is where confusion begins.

Not because something happened — but because **nothing did**.

When conflict arrives without cause, the body scrambles for logic. You start replaying moments, searching for what you missed, assuming the error must be yours.

SECTION 2

Charli did what she always did.

She softened her tone.
She explained herself.
She apologized for things she didn't understand.

And then Alfreda reached for the past.

Not last week.
Not yesterday.

Three years ago.
Four years ago.

Moments Charli barely remembered—offhand comments, old disagreements, things she thought had been talked through and released—were suddenly pulled forward, intact and sharp.

One by one, Alfreda laid them out.

You always do this.
This is who you've always been.
Remember when you said…
Remember how you acted…

Each memory delivered with the intensity of something that had just happened.

Charli wasn't responding to the present anymore.
She was on trial for the entire relationship.

COMMENTARY

This is how emotional time-travel works.

Nothing is resolved. Everything is stored.

Conflict isn't processed — it's archived. And when it reappears, it arrives fully charged, collapsing years into minutes.

SECTION 3

What Alfreda didn't know—and what Charli hadn't named yet—was that this pattern wasn't new to her body.

Charli had grown up inside it.

Her mother had done the same thing. Calm one moment, eruptive the next. Conversations that suddenly became interrogations. The past dragged into the present as proof of disrespect.

So when Alfreda did it, Charli didn't recognize it as harm.

It felt familiar.

And familiarity has a way of disguising danger.

COMMENTARY

This is where damage compounds.

When adulthood repeats childhood injury, the nervous system doesn't sound an alarm — it goes into survival mode.

You don't leave.
You adapt.

Not because you're weak, but because your body recognizes the rhythm.

SECTION 4

Over time, joy became conditional.

Peace felt temporary.
The connection felt fragile.

Charli never knew when the past would be brought out and used to dismantle whatever good existed in the moment.

What frightened her wasn't the arguments.

It was realizing that resentment had been quietly collected, preserved, and weaponized — not to resolve anything, but to control the present.

She didn't know what to call it.
She wasn't trying to diagnose anything.

She only knew she was exhausted from defending herself against history.

COMMENTARY

This dynamic doesn't teach communication.

It teaches hyper-vigilance.

You start monitoring tone, timing, and language — not to connect, but to avoid being ambushed by yesterday.

How Would You Have Handled This?

☐ **A.**
Apologized harder
and hoped it would finally stop.

☐ **B.**

Kept explaining yourself
to someone committed to misunderstanding.

☐ **C.**

Stayed because it felt familiar
and called that love.

☐ **D.**

Questioned your own memory
instead of the pattern.

☐ **E.**

Recognized that peace shouldn't require
emotional time travel.

Big Sis Reality Check

If the past is being used to destabilize the present,
healing isn't happening.

And if every argument requires a history lesson,
The issue isn't communication — it's containment.

Arguing with someone who keeps time-traveling is exhausting — every
fight needs a passport and a return ticket.

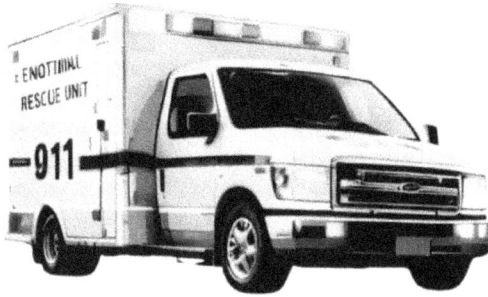

Big Sis Says

LOVE DOESN'T MAKE
YOU FOOLISH.
IGNORING THE
TRUTH DOES,
ESPECIALLY WHEN YOU
KEEP EXPLAINING AWAY
BEHAVIOUR THAT
KEEPS HURTING YOU.

Alex And Marie

When Love Has a Weight Limit

SECTION 1

Alex and Marie were the couple everyone admired.

Fit. Disciplined. Productive.
Their lives looked balanced and intentional, especially from the outside.
They worked hard, planned carefully, and moved through life like a team.

Then Marie gave birth to two things.

A beautiful baby.
And forty pounds she couldn't get rid of.

At first, no one said anything. Marie was healing. Tired. Adjusting to a body that didn't feel like hers anymore. She tried to eat well. She tried to exercise. She tried to stay positive.

Alex told himself he was being patient.

But patience quietly thinned.

COMMENTARY

This is where expectations go silent instead of being spoken.

Nothing is wrong *yet*.
But something is already shifting.

When attraction becomes conditional, distance starts forming long before anyone names it.

SECTION 2

The comments didn't arrive loudly.

They came disguised as concern.

Are you getting back into your routine?
You used to care more about yourself.
I'm just worried about you.

Marie felt it before she could explain it. She became more self-conscious. Less confident. More aware of her body in every room.

Food became comfort.
And then shame.
And then both at once.

Alex noticed — and pulled away.

He stayed later at work.
Then later than that.
Then sometimes not at all.

COMMENTARY

This is how abandonment often begins.

Not with leaving — but with withdrawing.
Not with cruelty — but with comparison.

When support disappears during vulnerability, the wound deepens quietly.

SECTION 3

Alex framed his distance as honesty.

I'm just not attracted anymore.
I need to be true to myself.
You've changed.

What he never said was this:

His love had conditions.
And Marie's body crossed one of them.

She internalized it as failure.
As a weakness.
As something she needed to fix.

And while she was drowning in self-blame, Alex kept disappearing.

COMMENTARY

When someone turns their preference into a verdict, the other person absorbs the damage.

This is how people learn to associate their body with abandonment — and call it self-improvement.

SECTION 4

Eventually, Alex stopped coming home.

Not suddenly.
Not dramatically.

Just gradually enough that Marie realized she was already alone.

What hurt most wasn't the weight.
It was discovering that love hadn't been tied to partnership — it had been tied to appearance.

COMMENTARY

Bodies change.

Pregnancy changes bodies.
Stress changes bodies.
Life changes bodies.

Love that can't survive transformation isn't love.

It's approval.

How Would You Have Handled This?

(Big Sis Manhattan Edition)

☐ **A.**
Blamed yourself
and tried to earn affection back.

☐ **B.**
Internalized the criticism
and called it motivation.

☐ **C.**
Ignored the withdrawal
until it became abandonment.

☐ **D.**
Questioned why your body
became a deal-breaker.

☐ **E.**
Recognized that love shouldn't expire
after childbirth.

Big Sis Reality Check

If someone's affection disappears when your body changes,
That's not honesty.

That's exposure.

And no one should have to earn love back
after surviving transformation.

If love has a weight limit, it's not love — it's a subscription with fine print.

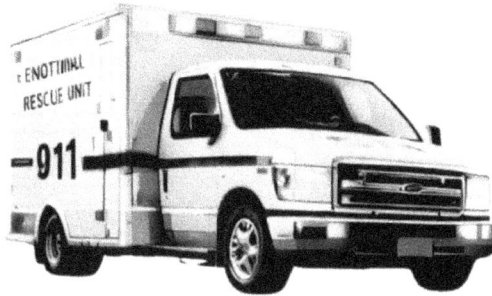

Big Sis Says

BE GENTLE WITH YOURSELF.
NEW CHALLENGES ILLICIT
NEW RESPONSES. WHEN
YOU KNOW BETTER YOU
WILL DO BETTER. UNTIL
THEN LOVE YOURSELF
THROUGH THE PAIN, GIVE
YOURSELF GRACE. LIFE IS A
LEARN-AS-WE-GO EVENT.

The Escape of the Narcissist

They don't leave you. They flee accountability.

SECTION 1

Here's the thing about narcissists:

They don't break up.
They escape — like fugitives who believe accountability is a maximum-security facility designed specifically to trap them.

They don't walk out the door.
They slide.
They slither.
They vanish.

And then they rewrite the story later like they barely survived *you*.

He didn't leave Marsha because he was finished.
He left because she was waking up.

Her questions were getting sharper.
Her memory was improving.
Her tolerance was thinning.

And narcissists cannot survive in clarity.

They need fog.
They need confusion.
They need a woman who doubts her own perception more than their behavior.

Marsha's light was becoming a problem.

28

COMMENTARY

This is the part people misunderstand:
A narcissist doesn't fear losing you.

They fear being seen.

SECTION 2

So he began the setup.

He picked fights Marsha didn't start.
Accused her of moods she wasn't in.
Blamed her for emotions he refused to manage.

When she asked for respect, he called her dramatic.
When she set a boundary, he called her controlling.
When she stayed calm, he accused her of being cold.

Nothing she did was ever right —
because the goal wasn't resolution.

The goal was destabilization.

COMMENTARY

Street definition time — because we're naming things now.

Narcissistic behavior looks like:
Turning your boundaries into "attacks"
Making you responsible for their reactions
Punishing you for emotional independence
Rewriting history so they're always misunderstood
Leaving suddenly so you're too stunned to question the truth

This isn't chaos.
It's a strategy.

SECTION 3

Then came the exit.

One morning, he left without explanation.
One afternoon, he stopped answering calls.
One evening, Marsha realized he wasn't coming back.

No closure.
No conversation.
No accountability.

Just absence.

And for a moment, it hurt like abandonment —
until clarity arrived.

COMMENTARY

Here's the reframe that saves women years of self-blame:

A narcissist leaving is not rejection.
It's avoidance.

They don't leave because you're unlovable.
They leave because you're no longer usable.

SECTION 4

Marsha didn't chase.
Didn't beg.
Didn't collapse into the familiar spiral of *What did I do wrong?*

She sat on the edge of her bed.
Wiped her face.
And said the words that changed everything:

"He didn't escape me.
He escaped accountability."

And suddenly — the grief softened.

Because what felt like loss
was actually release.

COMMENTARY

This is where freedom enters the room.

When you stop interpreting silence as punishment
and start seeing it as protection.

Sometimes God doesn't remove people gently.
Sometimes He evicts them.

SECTION 5

The quiet that followed wasn't empty.
It was peaceful.

No gaslighting.
No circular arguments.
No emotional whiplash.

Just space.
And clarity.
And the slow return of self-trust.

Marsha didn't gain closure from him.
She gained it from understanding the pattern.

COMMENTARY

Let this land where it needs to:

If someone disappears when you stop shrinking,
they didn't escape you.

They escaped exposure.

And trust —
Nothing of value ever runs from the truth.

How Would You Have Handled This?

☐ **A.**
Chased the explanation.
Replayed every conversation.
Called it "closure."

☐ **B.**
Blamed yourself
for not being "easier" to manipulate.

☐ **C.**
Waited for an apology
from someone allergic to accountability.

☐ **D.**
Tried to stay friends
with a person who treated honesty like a crime scene.

☐ **E.**
Accepted the disappearance,
blocked the exits,
and upgraded your peace package.

Big Sis Reality Check

If they vanish when you ask for clarity,
congratulations — the trash took itself out.

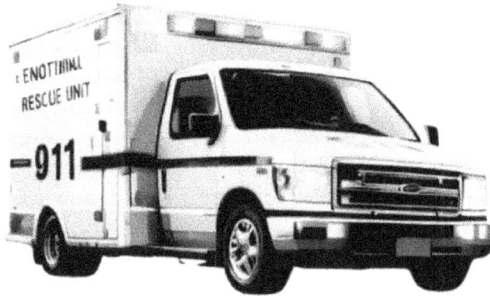

Big Sis Says

A NARCISSIST DOESN'T BREAK UP – THEY RELOCATE TO THEIR NEXT SUPPLY. LET THEM GO BE SOMEBODY ELSE'S LESSON.

Harvey, Elizabeth, And Anna

Let's Try Something New… or Someone New

SECTION 1

Harvey and Elizabeth were overachievers.

Careers thriving. Full schedules. Lives optimized.
From the outside, everything looked successful.

Except the bedroom.

Intimacy had faded quietly. Not because of betrayal or hatred—but boredom. Conversations turned sharp. Arguments became frequent and unfriendly, making tenderness feel awkward instead of natural.

Foreplay became impossible.
Not from lack of desire—but from unresolved tension.

Harvey decided the problem needed a solution.

Something bold.
Something exciting.
Something new.

COMMENTARY

This is where people mistake stimulation for connection.

When closeness fades, it's tempting to add excitement instead of slowing down to talk. Novelty feels easier than vulnerability.

SECTION 2

Harvey suggested bringing another person into their lives.

Not as an ending—he said—but as a spark.
A way to reconnect.
A way to feel alive again.

Elizabeth hesitated. She didn't feel jealous. She felt cautious. She sensed that something fundamental between them was being bypassed.

Eventually, she conceded.

At first, it worked.

Laughter returned. The tension lifted. Pressure eased.
The third person absorbed what Harvey and Elizabeth couldn't hold together.

But when the visits stopped, the silence returned.

COMMENTARY

This is the illusion of relief.

Distraction can feel like repair—but it never lasts. When the buffer disappears, the original problem waits exactly where it was left.

SECTION 3

Harvey suggested something bigger.

Anna moved in.

At first, it felt like balance. The house softened. Conversation flowed. For Elizabeth, it wasn't about desire—it was about companionship. Someone to talk to. Someone who listened.

Harvey enjoyed the image.
Two women beside him.
The attention.
The validation.

Until something shifted.

Suspicion crept in.

What are they doing when I'm not here?
Why do they seem closer to each other than to me?

COMMENTARY

This is where ego enters the room.

When novelty feeds power instead of partnership, insecurity follows. Control replaces curiosity. Trust becomes surveillance.

SECTION 4

Nothing was happening.

Elizabeth and Anna bonded like friends—talking, laughing, sharing space. There was no betrayal. No secrecy.

But Harvey's suspicion grew louder.

Accusations replaced dialogue.
Tension replaced ease. Eventually, Anna moved out.

And what moved in after her was resentment—thick, permanent, unresolved.

Harvey and Elizabeth were left with the truth they had avoided all along:

Adding someone new didn't fix what was broken.
It only delayed the reckoning.

COMMENTARY

This dynamic collapses because it was never about intimacy. It was about avoidance. When emotional distance exists, adding people multiplies the fracture instead of healing it.

HOW WOULD YOU HAVE HANDLED THIS?

☐ **A.**
Agreed to "something new"
instead of naming what was missing.

☐ **B.**
Used novelty
to avoid uncomfortable conversations.

☐ **C.**
Ignored the power imbalance
until resentment set in.

☐ **D.**
Confused distraction
with repair.

☐ **E.**
Stopped the experiment early
and demanded honesty instead.

BIG SIS REALITY CHECK

A third person cannot repair a relationship
that won't talk to itself.

If honesty can't survive between two people,
adding more only exposes the cracks.

Adding people to avoid a conversation is like pouring vinegar into milk and acting surprised when it curdles.

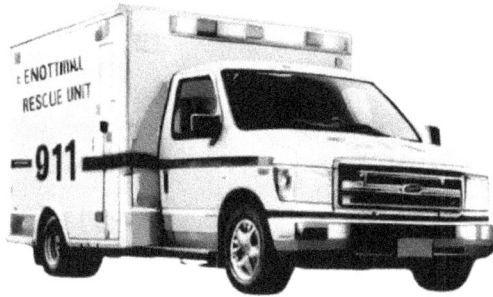

Big Sis Says

INSTEAD OF ASKING PEOPLE TO LOVE YOU BETTER, START ASKING YOURSELF WHY YOU STAYED WHEN YOUR NEEDS WERE TREATED LIKE INCONVENIENCES.

When Love Looks Right But Feels Wrong

SECTION 1

Jade and Sloane looked perfect together.
The kind of WLW couple strangers rooted for.

Matching mugs.
Shared playlists.
A dog named Mango who loved them like they invented sunlight.

From the outside, they were goals.

Inside the apartment?
The incompatibility was doing jumping jacks.

Jade was softness wrapped in tenderness.
Love notes tucked into bags.
Long talks that wandered instead of landed.

She needed closeness.
Emotional oxygen.
Room to feel.

Sloane loved Jade — deeply.
But she loved structure more.

Schedules.
Efficiency.
Clear roles.
Progress metrics disguised as romance.

Jade cried quietly.
Sloane offered "solutions."

Jade wanted stillness.
Sloane wanted strategy.

There was no villain here.
Just two good women speaking different emotional languages
and calling it compromise.

COMMENTARY

This is the part no one likes to name.

WLW relationships don't fail loudly.
They fail politely.

They fail through over-functioning.
Through emotional labor masquerading as loyalty.
Through *"we can fix this"* turning into *"I can survive this."*

Street definition time:

Woman-on-woman crime isn't betrayal.
It's two women slowly bleeding themselves dry
trying not to be the one who quits.

So they stay.

Because WLW love doesn't break up quickly.
It conducts a multi-year feasibility study.

They said:
"We've invested so much."
"It's just stress."
"This is a phase."
"All relationships take work."

But compatibility doesn't respond to effort.
It responds to alignment.

And alignment had already moved out.

SECTION 2 — The Shrinking & The Hardening

Jade started shrinking herself to keep the peace.
Lowered expectations.
Softer asks.
Quieter needs.

Sloane started hardening herself to maintain control.
More rules.
Less patience.
Tighter emotional budgets.

They still loved each other.

But love without compatibility turns into management.
And nobody wants to be audited at home.

One quiet morning, Jade stirred her tea like it owed her money.
Sloane scrolled her phone like it was a life raft.

And for the first time, they saw the same truth at the same time.

This love was real.
But the relationship was over.

COMMENTARY

This is the moment most people avoid.

Not because it's dramatic —
but because it's honest.

No screaming.
No betrayal.
No broken furniture.

Just the slow recognition
that love alone is not enough
when two nervous systems are incompatible.

Jade whispered,
"We're not happy, are we?"

Sloane exhaled,
"No... we're not."

That wasn't a failure.
That was maturity.

SECTION 3 — The Bravest Kind Of Love

They hugged —
not to hold on,
but to release.

Because sometimes the bravest love
is the love that stops negotiating its own unhappiness.

They didn't burn the house down.
They didn't villainize each other.

They chose clarity over endurance.

COMMENTARY

Big Sis clears her throat here.

Not every ending is a betrayal.
Some are just honest math.

And compatibility doesn't improve
with more meetings.

Besides…
even the best partnerships dissolve
when the culture no longer fits.

Bye, bitch. Bye.

HOW WOULD YOU HAVE HANDLED THIS?

☐ **A.**
Stayed longer.
Tried harder.
Scheduled another "check-in" about feelings.

☐ **B.**
Called incompatibility a "rough patch"
and kept submitting emotional expense reports.

☐ **C.**
Shrink-wrapped yourself into who they needed
and wondered why you couldn't breathe.

☐ **D.**
Held on for optics
because the mugs still matched.

☐ **E.**
Admitted love was real
but alignment had already moved out.

BIG SIS REALITY CHECK

If the relationship requires constant translation,
you're not partnered — you're negotiating.

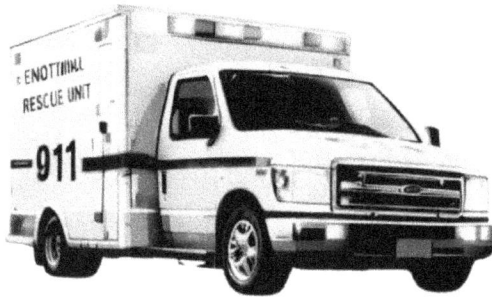

Big Sis Says

NOT EVERY BREAKUP
HAS A VILLAIN.
SOMETIMES LOVE JUST
EXPIRES – STOP
REHEATING WHAT GOD
UNPLUGGED.

Can You Love the Me You See?

SECTION 1 — Before The Mirror Spoke

Before the transition—
before hormones,
before doctors' appointments,
before the mirror finally told the truth—

Jordan and Maya were *that* couple.

Twelve years together.
The kind of relationship people used as proof that love could last.

Shared grocery lists.
Shared jokes no one else understood.
Shared silence that felt safe.

They built a life on familiarity.
And for a long time, that felt like enough.

Jordan had always known something was off.
Not broken—just unfinished.
Like living in a house where one room stayed locked.

Maya loved Jordan deeply.
She loved the consistency.
The predictability.
The version of Jordan she could name without thinking.

When Jordan finally said the words out loud—
"I'm transitioning"—

Maya didn't scream.
Didn't storm out.
Didn't say anything cruel.

She said,
"I want to support you." And she meant it.
At least… she thought she did.

SECTION 2 — When Support Meets Reality

Transition isn't one moment.
It's a series of mirrors you don't recognize right away.

Jordan changed slowly.
A new name.
New pronouns.
A body that finally felt like home.

Maya tried.
She really did.

But love started hesitating.

She paused before using Jordan's name.
Corrected herself too late.
Smiled with her mouth, not her eyes.

"I'm still me," Jordan would say softly.

Maya would nod.
But her body told a different story.

Hugs loosened.
Conversations shortened.
Affection felt… scheduled.

It wasn't hostility.
It was distance wearing politeness.

Jordan felt it everywhere—
in the way Maya stopped reaching first,
in how compliments disappeared,
in how intimacy became careful instead of connected.

Transition didn't just reshape Jordan's body.
It reshaped the relationship.

SECTION 3 — The Photograph

One quiet afternoon, Jordan walked into the bedroom and stopped cold.

Maya was sitting on the bed.
Holding an old photograph.

Pre-transition.
The version of Jordan she fell in love with.

Maya traced the jawline with her thumb.
Not longing.
Grief.

Jordan didn't interrupt.
Didn't accuse.
Didn't cry.

She just understood.

This wasn't adjustment.
This was mourning.

That night, Maya finally said what she'd been choking on for months:

"I love you…
but I don't know how to love the me I see when I look at you now."

It wasn't cruelty.
It was honesty.

And honesty still hurts when it tells the truth.

SECTION 4 — The Choice

Jordan packed slowly.

No slammed doors.
No screaming matches.
No villain speeches.

Just dignity.

"I won't shrink myself back into someone who made you comfortable,"
Jordan said.
"I deserve to be loved as I am... not tolerated as I become."

Maya cried like something precious had been taken from her.

But nothing was stolen.

Jordan didn't abandon Maya.
Jordan chose herself.

And that matters.

COMMENTARY — Big Sis Says

Not every breakup has a bad guy.

Sometimes love ends because one person grows
and the other can't follow without losing themselves.

That doesn't make Maya hateful.
It makes her honest.

And it doesn't make Jordan selfish.
It makes her brave.

You are not required to stay
where your evolution becomes someone else's grief.

Love that only works when you stay the same
isn't love—
it's nostalgia with benefits.

Besides…
If someone can only love you in past tense,
they're not meant for your future.

And no matter how much you miss them—
you can't move forward while being loved backward.

How Would You Have Handled This?

☐ **A.**
Delayed your transition
to keep the peace
and slowly disappeared anyway.

☐ **B.**
Accepted "support"
that felt more like supervision.

☐ **C.**
Stayed out of guilt
and called it loyalty.

☐ **D.**
Tried to make yourself lovable again
by becoming a memory.

☐ **E.**
Chose authenticity
even when it cost familiarity.

BIG SIS REALITY CHECK

If they can only love who you were,
they don't get access to who you're becoming.

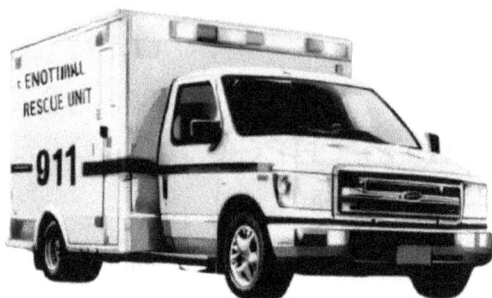

Big Sis Says

LOVE IS NOT
SUPPOSED TO
FEEL LIKE
YOU'RE
AUDITIONING
FOR A ROLE.

I'm Addicted to Her. She's Addicted to Gambling.

SECTION 1 — The Confusion

Janelle thought love was supposed to feel like a slow waltz—steady, rhythmic, predictable.

Loving Rhea felt like standing in a casino during an earthquake.

Flashing lights.
False hope.
Emotional overdraft.

They met on a random Tuesday—both dodging responsibilities, both hungry for distraction.

Rhea's smile was electric, the kind that made you feel chosen, lucky, special.

Janelle mistook adrenaline for chemistry.
She mistook chaos for passion.
She mistook intensity for intimacy.

At first, the gambling looked harmless.
Scratch-offs at the gas station.
A quick stop at the slots after dinner.

"Just for fun," Rhea said, laughing.

And casinos, like certain relationships, are designed the same way:
easy to enter, hard to leave,
and everything costs more than advertised.

SECTION 2 — The Pattern

Rhea wasn't addicted to money.
She was addicted to the *maybe*.

"Baby, I'm about to hit," became her love language.

Hope replaced plans.
Luck replaced responsibility.

When the lights got cut off the first time, Rhea romanticized it.
"Let's pretend we're camping."

By the second time, it was stress.
By the third, it was Janelle's fault.

"You don't believe in me."
"You're always so negative."
"If you had faith, this would work."

Bills stacked.
Cars disappeared.
Money vanished like it had legs.

And still—Janelle stayed.

Because addiction doesn't live alone.
Rhea was addicted to gambling.
Janelle was addicted to Rhea.

SECTION 3 — The Moment of Clarity

The final straw wasn't the money.
It was the look.

Janelle found Rhea at the casino late one night—
eyes glassy, jaw tight, hand slamming the spin button like she was trying
to win her soul back.

"Rhea," Janelle whispered, barely recognizing the woman she loved. "I'm losing myself trying to save you."

"Don't distract me!" Rhea snapped. "I'm about to hit!"

And in that moment, everything clicked.

Janelle wasn't Rhea's partner.
She wasn't Rhea's priority.
She wasn't even Rhea's problem.

She was Rhea's collateral damage.

SECTION 4 — The Exit

Janelle walked out crying.
Not for Rhea.
For herself.

For every boundary she bent.
For every bill she covered.
For every time she confused loyalty with self-erasure.

She finally understood the truth:

You cannot save someone who worships the gamble more than the love. You cannot compete with an addiction that promises hope without accountability.

And walking away wasn't betrayal.
It was survival.

COMMENTARY — Big Sis Says

Addiction doesn't always look like drugs or alcohol.
Sometimes it looks like hope dressed up as possibility.

And loving an addict doesn't make you weak.
But staying once you see the pattern
will cost you everything you didn't mean to gamble.

You are not required to bankrupt your life
just because someone else won't cash out.

Besides…
the house always wins.

And if you stay long enough—
you become the collateral, not the prize.

Bye, bitch. Bye.

How Would You Have Handled This?

☐ **A.**
Covered the bills.
Covered the lies.
Called it love.

☐ **B.**
Stayed for potential
and ignored the actual damage.

☐ **C.**
Believed "about to hit"
was a financial plan.

☐ **D.**
Tried to love someone sober
who was committed to chaos.

☐ **E.**
Left the table
before the house took everything.

Big Sis Reality Check

If you're betting your peace on someone else's addiction,
you're already losing.

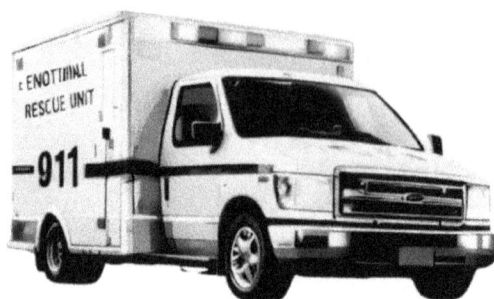

Big Sis Says

YOU DIDN'T BREAK
– YOU LEARNED
YOUR LIMIT.
CLOSURE ISN'T A
CONVERSATION.
IT'S A DECISION.

**Sex Doesn't Matter

*(...The Hell You Say)***

SECTION 1 — The Lie We Tell Out Loud

People love to act evolved about sex.

"Oh, we're spiritually connected."
"Oh, intimacy is deeper than the physical."
"Oh, sex isn't a priority anymore."

Baby... nothing exposes a relationship faster than a dry spell.

Let Big Sis introduce you to Desiree.

Desiree swore sex didn't matter.
She said it confidently.
Repeated it publicly.
Wore it like emotional enlightenment.

"We don't need sex to feel close," she'd say, chin high,
like she'd cracked some higher code of love.

And for a while, she believed it.

Because love wasn't the issue.
Malcolm was.

COMMENTARY

People don't downplay sex because they've evolved.
They downplay it because they're adapting.

Sometimes to distance.
Sometimes to denial.
Sometimes to survival.

SECTION 2 — The Shift

Malcolm didn't stop touching her gradually.
He stopped strategically.

A missed kiss here.
A pulled-away hug there.
A body that suddenly slept on the edge of the bed
like Desiree had an STD.

No fights.
No explanations.

Just absence.

At first, Desiree rationalized it.
"He's stressed."
"He's tired."
"Maybe I'm being dramatic."

But here's the thing Big Sis knows:
A woman always knows when she is no longer desired.

Not because of sex —
but because of avoidance.

COMMENTARY

Desire doesn't disappear quietly.
It leaves clues.

And the body notices what the mind tries to excuse.

SECTION 3 — The Moment It Breaks

The night everything shattered wasn't dramatic.

No screaming.
No accusations.

Desiree reached for him gently —
not aggressively,
not desperate,
just human.

Malcolm turned away.

Not asleep.
Not distracted.
Just uninterested.

And that cut deeper than rejection ever could.

Because sex wasn't the issue.
Being wanted was.

COMMENTARY

Rejection hurts.
Indifference rearranges your self-worth.

SECTION 4 — The Gaslight

When Desiree finally spoke up — calm, measured, honest —
Malcolm smirked.

"You're making sex into a bigger deal than it is," he said.
"Sex doesn't matter."

And in that moment, Desiree saw it clearly.

People only say *sex doesn't matter* when:
• they aren't giving it
• or they're getting it somewhere else
• or they're using deprivation as control

Sex isn't just physical.
It's validation.
It's connection.
It's confirmation.

And withholding it is never neutral.

COMMENTARY

If intimacy is used as leverage,
the relationship is already out of integrity.

SECTION 5 — The Exit

Desiree didn't argue.
She didn't beg for crumbs of intimacy.
She didn't audition for desire.

She packed her dignity.
Her lotion.
And the last shred of self-respect
she hadn't already talked herself out of.

Malcolm realized sex mattered
the moment she walked out the door.

Funny how clarity shows up late
but never lies.

<u>COMMENTARY — Big Sis Says</u>

Sex doesn't have to be constant.
But desire has to be present.

You don't owe anyone access to your body —
but you also don't owe anyone silence
when intimacy is weaponized.

Love without desire becomes roommates.
Desire without respect becomes damage.

And anyone who minimizes your need to feel wanted
is asking you to minimize yourself.

Besides…
If sex "doesn't matter,"
it shouldn't disappear only on your side of the bed.

How Would You Have Handled This?

☐ **A.**
Convinced yourself you were asking for too much
and called emotional starvation "growth."

☐ **B.**
Accepted the roommate upgrade
and pretended the bed wasn't cold.

☐ **C.**
Kept initiating
until rejection started feeling personal.

☐ **D.**
Believed "sex doesn't matter"
meant *your* desire didn't matter.

☐ **E.**

Chose self-respect,
left the dry spell behind,
and took your desire with you.

Big Sis Reality Check

If intimacy disappears but expectations don't,
you're not loved — you're managed.

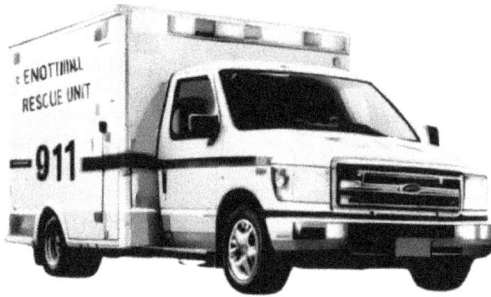

Big Sis Says

WHEN YOU KNOW BETTER, YOUR SPIRIT WON'T LET YOU DO WORSE. THAT'S NOT ATTITUDE – THAT'S GROWTH.

Everybody Had a Key

SECTION 1 — The Dream

By the time Naomi and Andre found each other, they weren't naïve.

Between them were six children, two demanding careers, two households of history, and enough lived experience to know love didn't survive on vibes alone.

They didn't dream small.
They dreamed strategic.

A blended family.
Shared responsibility.
A house loud with laughter and controlled chaos.

They believed love could organize itself
if everyone stayed committed.

That was their first mistake.

SECTION 2 — The Crowd

Love didn't enter quietly —
but neither did the audience.

Two sets of in-laws.
Two matriarchs.
Both convinced they were the final authority.

One believed tradition was law.
The other believed experience outranked consent.

Every decision became a discussion.
Every discussion became a verdict.

School choices.
Discipline.
Holidays.
Money.
Bedtimes.

Boundaries that never stood a chance.

Naomi felt judged before she spoke.
Andre felt emasculated without saying the word.

And the children?
They learned quickly who to run to
when the answer was "no."

SECTION 3 — The Strain

Work didn't pause.
Bills didn't wait.

Six children meant six schedules,
six emotional ecosystems,
six reasons someone was always tired.

Sex became something discussed, not practiced.
Rest became a luxury.
Silence became suspicious.

Naomi started feeling like a manager, not a wife.
Andre started feeling like an employee in his own home.

They loved each other — fiercely.
But love was being outvoted.

SECTION 4 — The Power Struggle

The breaking point wasn't loud.

It was a quiet Sunday.

Naomi stood in the kitchen, staring at a calendar covered in everyone else's handwriting.

Andre watched his mother rearrange furniture she didn't pay for.

And at that moment, something landed.

Not anger.
Clarity.

Their marriage wasn't failing.
It was overcrowded.

Too many opinions.
Too many access points.
Too many people with keys.

SECTION 5 — The Conversation

They didn't argue.

They sat on the edge of the bed —
exhausted, honest, unguarded.

"We're disappearing," Naomi said quietly.

Andre nodded.
"And everyone thinks they're helping."

That's when they made the decision.

Not to cut people off —
but to cut interference down.

They chose counseling.
They chose private decisions.
They chose delayed responses.
They chose each other in real time.

Some family members resisted.
Some guilt was deployed.
Some tears were strategic.

But the boundaries stayed.

COMMENTARY — Big Sis Says

Marriage doesn't collapse from lack of love.
It collapses from unmanaged access.

Support is invited.
Authority is earned.

And no one gets to run a household
they don't live in.

Blended families don't need more opinions —
They need clear leadership.

And that leadership must come from the couple.

Besides...
If everybody has a key to your marriage,
don't be surprised when privacy gets robbed.

Change the locks.
Keep the love.

How Would You Have Handled This?

☐ **A.**

Let everyone weigh in
and wondered why nothing ever felt settled.

☐ **B.**

Called interference "family support"
and slowly disappeared inside your own house.

☐ **C.**

Argued in private
but surrendered in public.

☐ **D.**

Tried to keep the peace
by sacrificing authority.

☐ **E.**

Locked the doors emotionally,
set boundaries clearly,
and remembered marriage isn't a group chat.

Big Sis Reality Check

If everybody has access to your marriage,
Nobody is responsible for protecting it.

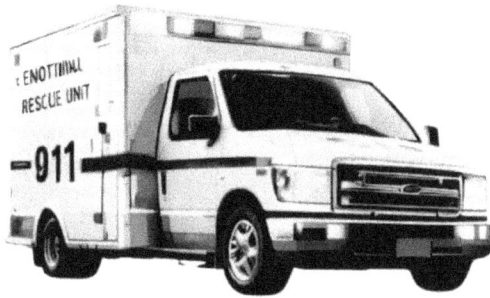

Big Sis Says

HEALING WILL
HAVE YOU GLIDING
PAST PEOPLE YOU
ONCE CRIED OVER.
THAT'S NOT SHADE
– THAT'S EVOLUTION.

Jordan and Marcus

Falling in Love With Potential

SECTION 1

Jordan didn't fall for Marcus because things were easy.

She fell because his life was hard.

He had stories—about setbacks, about being misunderstood, about how close he always was to things finally turning around. Jordan listened. She empathized. She admired his resilience.

Helping felt like bonding.

She covered small things at first.
Then bigger ones.

She encouraged him. Rewrote his résumé. Softened his edges in social spaces. Explained him to other people before he ever had to.

Marcus loved how patient she was.
How understanding.
How willing to see who he *could* be.

Jordan mistook gratitude for love.

COMMENTARY

This is where compassion quietly replaces compatibility.

When empathy leads the relationship, attraction can feel deep—even when effort isn't shared.

SECTION 2

Over time, Jordan noticed the imbalance.

The more she leaned in, the more Marcus leaned back.
The more she invested, the less he did.

Progress stalled.
Promises stayed abstract.

When Jordan finally asked for consistency—for clarity, for momentum—Marcus looked genuinely confused.

"I thought you understood me."

What he meant was: *I thought you'd keep carrying this.*

COMMENTARY

This is the cost of being the builder.

When one person becomes the engine of the relationship, the other never has to start theirs.

SECTION 3

Jordan began shrinking her expectations.

She stopped asking questions that made Marcus uncomfortable. She reframed disappointment as patience. She convinced herself that love meant waiting.

But waiting wasn't neutral.

It drained her.
It dimmed her confidence.
It turned hope into labor.

She wasn't in love with a partner anymore.

She was managing a project.

COMMENTARY

Potential is seductive because it feels hopeful.

But potential without action isn't promise—it's postponement.

SECTION 4

The realization arrived quietly.

Jordan wasn't choosing Marcus.
She was choosing who she believed he *might* become.

And while she waited, her own life stayed paused.

Letting go hurt—not because she lost him, but because she finally admitted how much of herself she had been giving away.

COMMENTARY

Love shouldn't require construction.

If you're constantly building the relationship alone, you're not partnered—you're employed.

How Would You Have Handled This?

☐ **A.**
Stayed patient
and kept believing effort would eventually match yours.

☐ **B.**

Mistook empathy
for intimacy.

☐ **C.**

Lowered expectations
and called it understanding.

☐ **D.**

Waited for potential
to turn into behavior.

☐ **E.**

Chose alignment
over hope.

Big Sis Reality Check

Potential is not a relationship plan.

If someone needs you to carry the future alone,
they're not ready to walk beside you.

Dating someone for their potential is like buying ingredients and
calling it dinner.

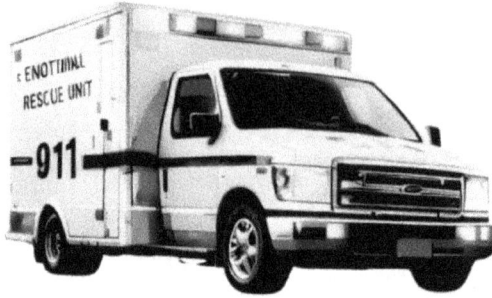

Big Sis Says

"CATCH A SALE,
CATCH A NAP,
CATCH A CLUE.
BUT WHATEVER YOU
DO – DON'T CATCH
A CASE
BEHIND A CLOWN."

When God, Therapy, And Blocking Meet

Pull up a chair.
This is the chapter where your spirit gets delivered.

Some of y'all don't need another prophecy.
You need a **boundary**.
You need a **therapist**.
And you need a **block button with a titanium hinge**.

This is the holy trinity of emotional survival:

God.
Therapy.
Blocking.

And when all three meet?
Peace gets promoted to management.

The Pre-Breakthrough: Confusion Masquerading As Comfort

She wasn't confused.

She just didn't want the truth to be true.

So she:

- rewrote the red flags,
- ignored the whispers,
- handed out *one more chances* like coupons at a grocery store.

Every time God sent a sign, she squinted.
Every time intuition screamed, she turned the volume down.
Every time therapy tried to help, she skipped the homework.

Sis wasn't stuck.
She was **stalling**.

The Quiet "Enough" That Saves Your Life

Healing didn't hit her loud.

It came like a soft sunrise.

A whisper inside said:

"Enough."

Not the cute kind.
Not the Instagram-caption kind.

The kind that sounds like:

- *I'm tired of being tired.*
- *I'm done babysitting grown people.*
- *I reject being anyone's emotional custodian.*

Her soul filed for emancipation.

God & Therapy Tag-Teaming Your Deliverance

Therapy said:
"You're not asking for too much. You're asking the wrong people."

God said:
"And didn't I tell you that already?"

Therapy gave her vocabulary.
God gave her backbone.
Blocking gave her peace.

Blocking Is Not Petty — It Is Spiritual Hygiene

People love to guilt-trip you out of protecting your peace.

"You're dramatic."
"You're mean."
"You're overreacting."

No.

A boundary only offends people who were benefiting from your lack of one.

Blocking is not hate.
Blocking is **self-love with a security badge**.

Sometimes the closure is simply:

Access denied.

The Big Sis Files

Attachment A: The Ministry of Blocking
Blocking can save lives — *yours*.
Stop resurrecting demons who drain your battery.

Attachment B: God Did Not Assign You to Be an Emotional EMT
Cease rushing to fix people who break on purpose.

Attachment C: Healing Comes With Receipts
"You didn't lose them — you released them."
"They didn't fall away — they fell off."

Attachment D: Heaven Applauds Boundaries
Your peace gets clapped for in realms you cannot see.

Final Word

Blocking is a boundary.
Therapy is a tool.
God is the strategy.

You are the prize.

And just in case you needed permission:

Bye Bitch Bye.

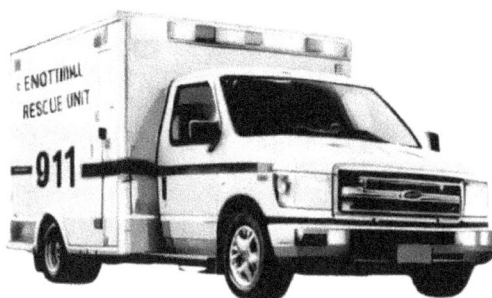

Big Sis Says

**CREATE YOUR
SELF-RESCUE PLAN.
YOU HAVE
A WINNING TEAM,
GOD,
THERAPY,
AND BOUNDARIES.**

The Day You Replace Why with How Is the Day You Get Free

WHY is the road you take when you're tired, confused, hurting, and desperate for a reason that will magically make the pain make sense.

Spoiler alert: It never comes.

WHY did they leave?

WHY did they lie?

WHY wasn't I enough?

WHY did I stay?

WHY didn't they love me the way I loved them?

WHY is a long, winding, nasty, never-ending road.

A treadmill with emotional potholes.

A spiritual dead end with good lighting.

WHY feels productive — but all it really does is loop you back into the very moment you survived.

WHY:

- replays the trauma in slow-motion, HD, surround sound
- tricks you into thinking closure lives in their explanation
- convinces you that if you just understood, you'd finally be free
- keeps feeding your heartbreak tiny snacks of hope

But WHY never heals.

WHY just exhausts.

Here's the truth Big Sis needs you to catch in your chest:

HOW is where your comeback begins.

HOW asks:

- HOW do I rebuild myself?
- HOW do I protect my peace?
- HOW do I end repeating emotional patterns?
- HOW do I love myself better than they ever could?
- HOW do I move forward without carrying what broke me?

WHY keeps you in the past.

HOW creates the future.

WHY circles the wound.

HOW stitches it closed.

WHY is survival mode.

HOW is transformation.

The day you shift from WHY to HOW —that's the day your healing rejects crawling and starts RUNNING.

Sis, let me tell you something straight:
Trauma may have slowed you down, but it did **not** take you out.
You're standing here with a book in your hand because there is still a fire in you that refuses to die.
That fire is your power — and now it's time to use it.

Every chapter in this book asked you to look at life without flinching.
You faced the patterns, the heartbreaks, the heartbreakers, the moments

you blamed yourself, and the moments you almost forgot who you were. But look at you — still here, still healing, still rising.

Now I want you to pause and ask yourself three simple, life-shifting questions:

1. How did what happened to you make you feel?

Not how you *pretended* to feel.
Not how you *thought* you were supposed to feel.
But how you really, deeply, honestly felt inside your bones.

2. How do you feel now, standing on the other side of that truth?

Maybe lighter.
Maybe angry.Maybe hopeful.
Maybe still figuring it out — and that's okay.
Awareness is progress.
Progress is power.

3. How do you *want* to feel moving forward?

Free?
Seen?
Safe?
Loved?
Unapologetically yourself?
Whatever your answer is — that becomes your next destination.

Trauma tries to convince you that your story is over.
But Big Sis is here to remind you:
Your story is just beginning, and this time *you* hold the pen.

You're not surviving anymore.
You're awakening.
You're gathering your strength, your standards, your boundaries, your voice — and you're stepping into the kind of life that honors your worth.

Turning trauma into power doesn't happen in one night.
It happens one decision at a time:

- The decision to **no longer chase** people who don't choose you.
- The decision to **no longer shrink** to make others feel comfortable.
- The decision to **no longer apologize** for wanting peace.
- The decision to **listen to your own spirit** before you listen to anyone else.

Sis, you don't need closure.
You need **clarity.**
And now you have it.

You've walked through the fire.
Now it's time to **rise above the smoke** and build a life that matches who you're becoming — not who you were forced to be.

Your trauma may have been the introduction,
but **your power is the rest of the story.**

And Big Sis is right here, cheering for every chapter you write next.

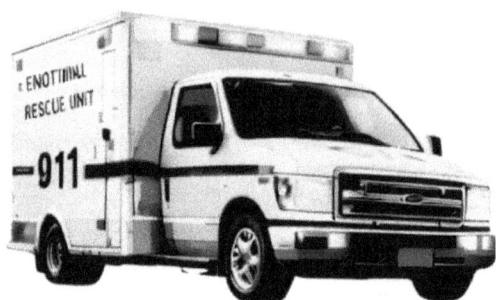

Big Sis Says

CHOOSING YOU IS
A RESURRECTION.
BABY, LOOK AT YOU –
ALIVE, HEALING,
AND UNAVAILABLE
FOR ANYTHING
LESS.

What You Just Survived (And What Comes Next)**

If you made it this far, pause.

Not because you're tired —
but because something inside you is awake.

These stories weren't meant to entertain you.
They were meant to mirror you.

Different names.
Different cities.
Different dynamics.

Same patterns.

And before we go any further, Big Sis needs to say this clearly:

Nothing you read means you failed.
It means you recognized something.

That's not weakness.
That's awareness.

The Common Thread You May Have Missed

Every story you read looked different on the surface.

Cheating.
Addiction.
Power shifts.
Family interference.
Sex withheld.

Identity evolution.
Emotional abandonment.
Control disguised as love.

But underneath?

The same quiet erosion:

People losing themselves while trying to save relationships.
People confuse loyalty with self-erasure.
People stayed too long because leaving felt harder than shrinking.

No one in these stories was stupid.
No one was unlovable.
No one "should've known better."

They just didn't have tools yet.

Why This Part of the Book Exists

You've now seen what happens when:

- boundaries are delayed
- discernment is ignored
- desire is dismissed
- accountability is avoided
- communication is replaced with endurance

And here's the part nobody says out loud:

Love alone is not a skill set.

Hope is not a strategy.
Patience is not protection.
And commitment without clarity becomes captivity.

That doesn't mean relationships are doomed.

It means they require management, not martyrdom.

Single, Partnered, Or Complicated — This Part Is for You

Whether you're:

- single and healing
- partnered and overwhelmed
- married and renegotiating
- blended and stretched thin
- questioning everything but still hopeful

Segment II is not about "fixing" you.

It's about equipping you.

Because self-rescue is not selfish.
It's sustainable.

And you don't need a breakup to deserve better tools.

What Changes Now

Up to this point, the stories showed you what happens.

What comes next shows you what to do.

Not commandments.
Not ultimatums.
Not "just leave."

But real-life methods for:

- staying whole while loving others
- setting boundaries without burning bridges
- communicating needs without apologizing for them

- managing shared lives without losing your identity
- recognizing when to repair — and when to release

These are not theories.

They are practices.

Big Sis Promise

This next segment won't shame you.
It won't rush you.
It won't tell you what choice to make.

It will teach you how to choose yourself inside any outcome.

Because the goal isn't perfection.

The goal is clarity, power, and choice —
so no matter what your relationship status says,
you remain intact.

The Reward

If these stories stirred something —
That means you're ready.

Ready to stop surviving relationships.
Ready to stop auditioning for love.
Ready to stop losing yourself in shared lives.

You don't need a new partner.

You need new skills.

Let's build them.

The Big Sis Self-Rescue Manifesto

(Read This When You Feel Yourself Slipping)

This is not a rulebook.
This is a reminder.

You are not here because you failed at love.
You are here because you survived it.

You are allowed to outgrow people who only knew the broken version of you.
You are allowed to choose peace without explaining yourself.
You are allowed to change your mind when new information arrives.

This manifesto exists for the moments when:

- your emotions start negotiating your boundaries,
- nostalgia tries to rewrite history,
- loneliness pretends to be love,
- or guilt shows up dressed as loyalty.

Read this slowly.
Return as needed.

I Will No Longer Abandon Myself to Keep Anyone

I will not shrink to make chaos comfortable.
I will not stay silent to preserve someone else's peace.
I will not explain my worth to people who benefit from misunderstanding me.

Love that costs me my nervous system is not love.
It's a debt.

I Will Trust What My Body and Spirit Are Telling Me

If my chest tightens, I will pause.
If my stomach knots, I will listen.
If my peace disappears, I will investigate.

My intuition does not need permission to speak.
It needs room.

I Will Not Confuse Attention with Affection

Consistency Is My New requirement.
Safety is my new standard.
Reciprocity is non-negotiable.

I am no longer impressed by charm without character
or promises without presence.

I Will Stop Chasing Closure from People Who Ran from Accountability

I release the need to be understood by those committed to misunderstanding me.
I do not need their apology to heal.
I do not need their acknowledgment to move forward.

Some doors close because they were never meant to be homes.

I Will Choose Response Over Reaction

I will not let my first emotion make my final decision.
I will pause before I pursue.
I will breathe before I explain.
I will ground before I engage.

My emotions inform me — they do not control me.

I Will Honor My Healing — Even When It Feels Uncomfortable

Healing may make me unfamiliar to people who preferred me wounded.
Healing may cost me relationships built on access instead of respect.
Healing may require me to sit alone before I sit aligned.

That is not a loss.
That is refinement.

I Am The Prize — And I Will Move Like It

I do not audition for love.
I do not beg for effort.
I do not negotiate my boundaries.

I choose people who choose me.
I build a life that includes me.
I protect my peace like it is sacred — because it is.

Final Declaration

I commit to living in alignment with who I am becoming —
not who I had to be to survive.

I do not go backwards.
I do not explain exits.
I do not stay where my spirit feels unsafe.

This is not hardness.
This is clarity.

This is Big Sis Energy.
And I stand in it — fully.

SEGMENT II
DISRUPTING THE PATTERN

Turning Trauma Into Power

Disrupting The Pattern
*Turning Trauma Into Power***

Recognition is only the first step.

Patterns don't end because you notice them.
They end when you **interrupt** them.

This section is not about revisiting the story.
It's about breaking the mental habits that kept you inside it.

Most people don't stay in unhealthy dynamics because they don't know better.
They stay because they were trained to override themselves.

To explain instead of feel.
To accommodate instead of pause.
To keep going instead of checking in.

Segment II slows that conditioning down.

Here, we stop rehearsing what happened.
We begin paying attention to **what it did to you**.

This is where deprogramming begins —
not by changing the past,
but by reclaiming authority over your inner state.

Read slowly.
Notice resistance.

That's not discomfort.
That's the pattern loosening its grip.

**What Happened

Understanding What Just Happened to You**

Losing someone suddenly — someone you trusted, invested in, and built a life around — can hit your spirit like a storm you never saw coming.

This isn't just emotional pain.
It's **full-body shock**.

The kind that rattles your confidence, your peace, and your sense of stability.

And here's what many women don't realize: A breakup can function like **trauma**.

Not because you're fragile —
but because the impact was that deep.

You didn't just lose a person.
You lost a rhythm.
A routine.
A future you were quietly planning.

When all of that collapses at once, your nervous system does what any system does after sudden impact:

It tries to protect you.

Common Trauma Responses After A Painful Breakup

1. Your mind replays the pain on a loop.

Flashbacks.
Triggers.
Overthinking at 2 a.m.

This isn't obsession.
It's your brain trying to create meaning where none was given.

2. Abandonment fear shows up uninvited.

You might cling.
You might shut down.
You might do both.

That's not weakness —
that's the body bracing for another hit.

3. Trust becomes complicated.

Not because you don't want love —
but because vulnerability now feels like walking into a room without walls.

4. Your self-esteem takes a hit.

You question your worth.
You replay conversations.
You wonder what you missed.

Please hear this clearly:
Your worth was never attached to who walked away.

5. Your emotions refuse to stay organized.

Crying.
Numbness.
Irritability.
Exhaustion.

All normal responses to emotional shock.

If The Impact Goes Unaddressed

When emotional injury isn't tended to, it doesn't disappear —
it just goes underground.

Here's how it shows up later:

1. Your mind stays tired.

Anxiety.
Low mood.
Hopelessness. Not because of the breakup itself —
but because you're carrying an untreated wound.

2. Patterns quietly repeat.

You chase what feels familiar — even if it hurts.
Or you sabotage new connections because pain feels predictable.

3. Coping gets complicated.

Emotional eating.
Drinking.
Oversleeping.
Fixating.
Scrolling.
Obsessing.

Not "bad behavior."

Human behavior. Your system asking for relief.

Big Sis Says

Nothing is wrong with you.

What you're experiencing makes sense given what you survived.

This section isn't here to diagnose you.
It's here to **ground you**.

Because understanding what happened to you
is the first step toward deciding
what happens *next*.

And you don't need to rush that decision.

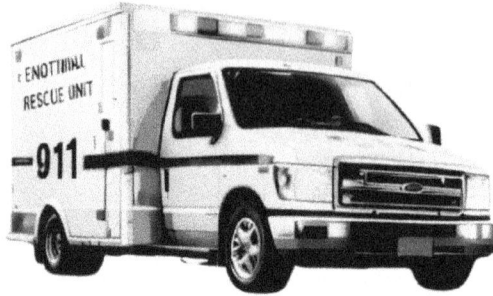

Big Sis Says

STOP REWRITING THE
STORY TO MAKE IT MAKE
SENSE.
WHAT HAPPENED...
HAPPENED.
AND THE MOMENT YOU
TELL THE TRUTH
WITHOUT SOFTENING IT,
YOUR HEALING FINALLY
HAS SOMEWHERE
TO START.

When Goodbye Saves Your Life

Why walking away is sometimes the sanest, bravest, most self-loving thing you can do

There comes a moment in every woman's story
when the word *goodbye* starts sounding like **oxygen**.

Because the truth is this:

We don't walk away because we're weak.
We walk away because we finally understand that love
should not require us to **die in installments**.

And many of us stayed longer than we should have, didn't we?

We stayed because:

- we didn't want to be seen as quitters,
- we believed *a little more time* could fix everything,
- we confused loyalty with abandoning our own needs,
- and sometimes… we stayed because healing ourselves felt harder than rescuing someone who wasn't ready to be saved.

Then one day — quiet, holy, terrifying —
your spirit whispers:

**"This isn't love anymore.
This is CPR on a relationship that flatlined seasons ago."**

And suddenly, goodbye stops sounding like an ending.

It becomes a **lifeline**.

What Walking Away Really Looks Like

Walking away is rarely dramatic.

It's not slammed doors or final showdowns.
It's quieter than that.
More honest.
More sacred.

It's the stillness of someone choosing themselves
without apology.

Goodbye is the morning you wake up and realize:

- you want peace more than passion,
- consistency more than chaos,
- reciprocity more than fantasy,
- freedom more than familiar pain.

Goodbye is the first boundary you set
for the version of you who has been waiting
behind your courage.

What You Reclaim When You Leave

Here's the part few people talk about:

You don't lose power by leaving.
You **reclaim** it.

You stop begging people to show up.
You stop negotiating your worth.
You stop performing for love.

You end offering discounts
on a heart that cost you everything to rebuild.

And one day — with distance, clarity, and steadier ground —
you look back at the woman you were and think:

"I almost lost myself
trying to keep the wrong story alive."

Goodbye is not the end of your life.

It is the beginning of the life
you were always meant to have.

And yes — it is beautiful.

Because there is nothing more powerful
than a woman who chooses herself
with clarity and conviction.

If you feel this truth rising in your chest,
let it rise.

That's not sadness.

That's **awakening**.
That's your power remembering its way home.

**UNIVERSAL COMMENTARY

When Heartbreak Comes From Pressure**

There's a kind of heartbreak women rarely talk about —
not caused by betrayal or deceit,
but by **pressure**.

Not cheating.
Not lies.
Not incompatibility.

Pressure.

Pressure from society.
From family.
From religion.
From reputation, culture, politics —
voices so loud they drown out what someone knows is true.

Some women don't lose love because love faded.
They lose love because their partner panicked
under the weight of other people's expectations.

Fear pretended to be clarity.
Fear dressed itself up as responsibility.
Fear sounded like maturity.

And this happens across every kind of relationship:

- successful women labeled "too much,"
- queer women whose partners fold under family judgment,
- interracial, interfaith, intercultural couples silenced by shame,
- women abandoned under religious or community pressure,
- trans women and men left behind to avoid discomfort or scrutiny.

Here is the truth that stings — and heals:

You were not left because you were unworthy.
You were left because they were afraid.

That kind of abandonment cuts deep.
It doesn't just wound the heart —
it injures identity.

And healing begins here:

You cannot shrink yourself
to fit inside someone else's courage.

You cannot keep alive a love
suffocating under other people's opinions.

You can only save **you**.

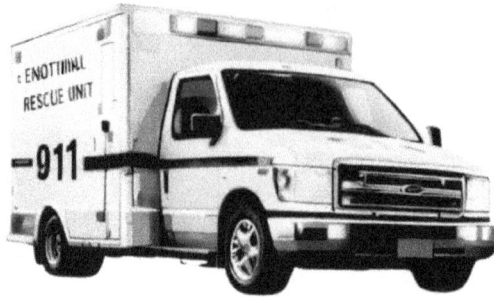

Big Sis Says

SOME GOODBYES
DON'T BREAK YOU –
THEY RESCUE YOU.
STOP GRIEVING THE
LOSS OF A PERSON.
GOD, YOUR GUT, AND
THE RED FLAGS TRIED
TO ESCORT OUT
MONTHS AGO.

Rise Above Emotions

The Chapter That Teaches You How to Notice When Your Feelings Are Driving the Car

Have you ever noticed how emotions act like toddlers in the back seat?
Loud.
Demanding.
Unbuckled.
Throwing snacks.
Reaching for a steering wheel they have no business touching.

That's the real problem —
We keep letting our emotions drive.
And they don't even have a license.

Don't blame yourself.
Most of us were raised to "get over it," "stay strong," "pray it away," or "stop being dramatic."
Nobody taught us how to *feel* without letting the feeling take over.

This chapter fixes that.

This is where you learn how to cease reacting from emotional panic and start responding from emotional power.

Because of your emotions?
They're messengers.
Not dictators.

Let's talk about it.

1. The Truth About Emotions

Emotions are not the enemy.
Unmanaged emotions are.

Feelings aren't facts —
they're information.
Signals.
Indicators.

Just because you *felt* it
doesn't mean it's the truth about you.

Sometimes your emotions are describing now.
Sometimes they're describing then,
And sometimes they're just repeating a fear-filled bedtime story your
nervous system memorized years ago.

Overwhelm doesn't mean you're broken.
It means you're human.

Rise Above Emotions is not about numbing or pretending.
It's about learning to say:

"This is a trigger."
"This is fear talking."
"This is old pain acting like new truth."
"This is grief — not guidance."
"This is abandonment history, not current reality."

When you can name what you're feeling,
you can overcome being controlled by what you're feeling.

That's emotional freedom.

2. Emotional Weather vs. Emotional Identity

Big Sis truth:
What you feel is not who you are.

Read that again.
Let it sink.

Your emotions are weather — constantly shifting.
A storm today.
Sun tomorrow.
Fog next week.
A little unexpected heat when the wrong person texts "hey stranger."

But who you *are*?
That's steady.
That's anchored.
That's not up for daily negotiations.

You're not "an anxious person."
You are a person *experiencing* anxiety.

You're not "unlovable."
You are a person *experiencing* heartbreak.

You're not "weak."
You are a person *experiencing* a trigger.

Identity is permanent.
The weather is temporary.

Most of us get in trouble because we confuse the two.

Not anymore.

3. Don't Declare the First Emotion a Winner

The first emotion is usually the loudest
and the least accurate.

Panic.
Clinging.
Anger.
Self-doubt.
Fantasy.
Rumination.
"I miss them"...
when what you really miss is the version of them you created in your
head.

Here's the rule:

Never make a decision from the first emotion.

Ever.

Pause.
Breathe.
Let the truth catch up.
It always arrives more quietly.

Rising above emotions means checking your internal weather
before you run into another storm you could have avoided.

When Fear Is Information
(Not Overreaction)

A Necessary Safety Note

Big Sis needs to say this clearly and responsibly:

Not every fear is emotional noise.
Some fear is **data**.

There is a dangerous myth that healing means staying calm at all costs.
That if you're afraid, you're "triggered," "dramatic," or "letting emotions run the show."

That is not true.

Sometimes fear isn't coming from your past.
It's coming from **pattern recognition**.

Especially when it comes to abusive or controlling relationships, the most dangerous moment is often **after** you leave — not before.

Why?

Because abuse was never about love.
It was about **control**.

And when control is lost, some people escalate.

That escalation can look like:

- stalking disguised as "checking on you,"
- harassment masked as "closure,"
- threats dressed up as "concern,"
- manipulation through money, the courts, or the children,

113

- sudden remorse that feels urgent, intense, and destabilizing.

If you've recently left — or are planning to leave — someone who scared you, intimidated you, or tried to control your choices, hear this:

Rising above emotions does not mean minimizing danger.
It means responding *wisely* instead of impulsively.

Courage without a plan is not strength.
It's exposure.

If your body feels tense, alert, watchful — don't shame it.
Your nervous system may be doing its job.

This is where emotional power looks like:

- telling someone what's happening instead of carrying it alone,
- working with an advocate or professional who understands post-separation abuse,
- documenting, planning, protecting, not provoking,
- choosing safety over speed.

You are not "weak" for being cautious.
You are **intelligent**.

And here is the Big Sis truth that matters most:

Healing is not just about calming your emotions.
It's about **keeping yourself alive long enough to enjoy the peace you're building**.

If you need immediate support, reach out to people trained for this moment — not just people who mean well.

You deserve safety *and* serenity.
One does not cancel the other.

4. Emotional Detox: What It Really Means

You can't rise above emotions
when you're carrying everybody else's.

So many women are holding:

someone else's guilt
someone else's insecurities
someone else's expectations
someone else's disappointment
someone else's judgment
someone else's fear

No wonder you're tired.

Emotional detox does not mean cutting everybody off.
It means returning what was never yours to keep.

Say this with me:

"This feeling is real, but it does not belong to me."

That's how you rise.

5. Emotional Maturity — The Big Sis Definition

Emotional maturity is not about being unbothered.
Social media lied.

Emotional maturity is:

honoring your peace above your pride
choosing clarity before conflict
telling the truth without weaponizing your wounds
letting people go without closing your heart
pausing instead of reacting
responding from wisdom instead of injury

refusing to chase anyone who walked away
no longer shrinking yourself to make chaos comfortable

Maturity is when your emotions advise your decisions
but no longer control them.

6. The Three Questions That Save Your Life

These questions are the emotional reset button of the G.A.G. Method:

1. How did the event make me feel?
Name it.
Own it.
Release it.

2. How do I feel now?
What part of you is still carrying the wound?

3. How do I want to feel?
This is where healing transitions from reaction to choice.

Rising above emotions isn't magic.
It's a method.
A practice.
A discipline that becomes a lifestyle.

And this —
this right here —
is the chapter where you finally take your feelings out of the driver's seat
and put yourself back behind the wheel.

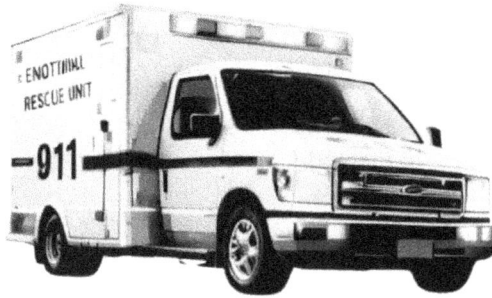

Big Sis Says

YOUR EMOTIONS ARE VALID, BUT THEY ARE NOT RELIABLE GPS. RISE ABOVE THE STORM LONG ENOUGH TO SEE THE LESSON, NOT JUST THE LIGHTNING.

Waiting Is an Acquired Taste

Waiting is not natural — it's learned.
It's like kale, budgeting, sunscreen, and telling people "no" without writing a four-part apology afterward.

We weren't raised to wait.
We were raised to:

- hurry so nobody thinks we're lazy,
- settle so nobody calls us picky,
- forgive so nobody calls us bitter,
- keep quiet so nobody calls us difficult,
- stay loyal so nobody calls us ungrateful.

But waiting?
Waiting requires a strength no one taught us.

Waiting feels like doing nothing —
but it is everything.

It's sitting with yourself long enough to hear your own spirit speak.
It's letting the emotional storm pass so you don't confuse panic with intuition.
It's giving your heart time to catch up to your wisdom.

Here's the truth that saves people from repeated heartbreak:

Most of us weren't choosing partners…
we were choosing relief.

Relief from loneliness.
Relief from silence.

Relief from feeling unchosen.
Relief from the fear that time is running out.

Healing requires slowing down long enough to separate relief from real connection.

Because real connection isn't urgent.
It doesn't demand panic.
It doesn't make you abandon your values in exchange for companionship.

Waiting is an acquired taste because it asks us to unlearn "desperation decisions."

Those choices we made when:

- our self-esteem was on clearance,
- our boundaries were optional,
- our trauma was louder than our logic,
- our loneliness was mistaken for chemistry,
- our unhealed self was selecting partners on our behalf.

You cannot heal in the morning and choose chaos later that afternoon.
Healing requires consistency, discipline, restraint, and intention.

And yes — patience is uncomfortable.
You will feel restless.
Your old habits will invite you back.
Your loneliness will lie to you.
Your ego will panic.
Your trauma bond will whisper, *"Just call them."*

Sometimes it's like bleeding hemorrhoids leaving you with intense pain and discomfort.

But hear this:

Healing is learning not to RSVP to every emotional craving.

Some urges exist only to test whether you've outgrown what once broke you.

When you truly wait, something shifts:

1. Clarity replaces craving.

You see the difference between attention and intention.

2. Your intuition becomes audible.

No more static, no more guessing.

3. You attract people who match your healed self.

Alignment opens doors urgency could never unlock.

4. You reject emotional crumbs.

Hunger is not a reason to eat poison.

5. You refuse to negotiate your worth.

Worth isn't determined by who chooses you.
It's revealed by who you refuse to choose again.

Waiting is not punishment — it is preparation.

Preparation for a partner who:

- respects boundaries on the first try,
- doesn't weaponize your vulnerability,
- doesn't need emotional babysitting,
- chooses you consistently,
- loves you in verbs, not vague promises.

Preparation for a future where you aren't drowning in emotional debt.
Preparation for a life where auditioning for roles you already qualify for
is no longer an option

Waiting reveals who you really are.

Are you patient, or do you self-sabotage?
Are you discerning, or do you panic-pick?
Are you healed, or have you only learned the language of healing?

Waiting exposes the truth —
and truth is the sharpest filter you'll ever use.

Waiting is an acquired taste — but so is self-worth.

And once you acquire it?

You **no longer crave** what broke you.

You **no longer chase** what drains you.

You **no longer tolerate** what triggers you.

You **no longer desire** what dishonored you.

You **no longer beg** for what life has already removed.

You **no longer accept** love that requires you to betray yourself.

Your healed self deserves a healed match —
not a project, a placeholder, or a panic purchase.

You deserve someone your future self will thank you for choosing.

Big Sis Says…

If waiting feels uncomfortable,
that's because your healed self is stepping into territory
your unhealed self didn't believe you'd ever reach.

Let it stretch.
Let it feel new.
Let it transform you.

Waiting is the price of admission for the life you prayed to live.
And you are worth the investment.

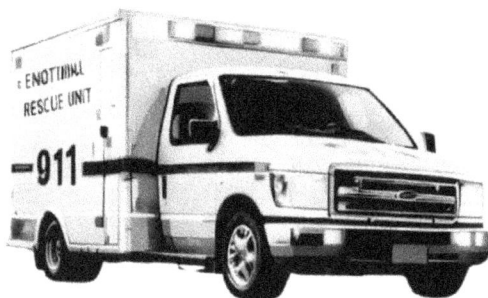

Big Sis Says

WAITING ISN'T PUNISHMENT – IT'S PREPARATION. ELEVATION REQUIRES PATIENCE YOUR OLD SELF DIDN'T HAVE. LET THE VERSION OF YOU THAT'S COMING TEACH YOU HOW TO WAIT WELL.

"The Version of Me You Knew Is Retired"

Let's land this chapter exactly where your power lives.

You didn't walk through all that fire
just to go back to the same smoke.

You didn't bleed, cry, reflect, journal, pray, block, unlearn, relearn, fall
apart, rebuild, rise again, straighten your crown, and fix your edges
just to return to the kind of people who only loved the broken version
of you.

Let Big Sis say this gently but firmly:

> What's the point of doing all this healing
> if you're gonna go back to the kind of love
> that required you to stay wounded?

Healing is not about becoming "better for them."
Healing is about becoming whole for you.

And once you become whole?

Your appetite changes.
Your tolerance changes.
Your standards change.
Your soul changes.
Your energy shifts.
Your spirit levels up.

And — your heart becomes too expensive
for discount-level love.

Healing isn't a quick fix. It's a spiritual realignment.

You start to want:

- peace more than attention
- consistency more than chemistry
- reciprocity more than romance
- emotional safety more than sweet talk
- presence more than promises

You learn to choose who chooses you.
Not the fantasy version of you,
but the healed, raw, still-evolving, beautifully human you.

A healed woman becomes her own filter.

And suddenly?

Some people won't make it through.
Not because they're "bad"…
but because they don't meet the requirements of your healed self.

And let Big Sis remind you:

> The version of you that worked for them
> no longer exists.

**Healing is a bridge.

Don't build the bridge and go backwards.**

You didn't claw your way out of pain
to settle for a relationship that keeps you questioning your worth.

You didn't learn your patterns
to ignore your intuition.

You didn't rise above your triggers
to fall for their potential.

You didn't break cycles
to create new ones with the same type of soul.

**The point of healing is this:

You get to choose better — not repeat worse.**

You get to wait.
You get to be selective.
You get to require what you deserve.
You get to say "no" without guilt
and "yes" without fear.

You get to meet someone who speaks the language of your healed heart.

And trust Big Sis…
that person exists.

But you'll miss them if you keep running back to the ones who only saw
your unhealed self.

So stand still.
Stay grounded.
Stay aligned.
Stay patient.

Healed love arrives when healed you is present.

Now breathe.
Receive that.
And walk out of this chapter knowing:

Your healing was not a detour —
it was preparation for someone who can meet you where you've risen.

You don't need to rush healed love.
You don't need to explain your standards.
You don't need to convince anyone you've changed.

Your peace will speak for you.

And when the old patterns knock —
because they will —
you'll recognize them not with panic,
but with clarity.

You won't argue.
You won't negotiate.
You won't romanticize.

You'll simply say:
"That no longer works for who I am."

That's healing in motion.
That's growth with boundaries.
That's love that doesn't require you to disappear.

Close this chapter knowing this:
You didn't heal to be chosen.
You healed to **choose**.

And you're choosing differently now.

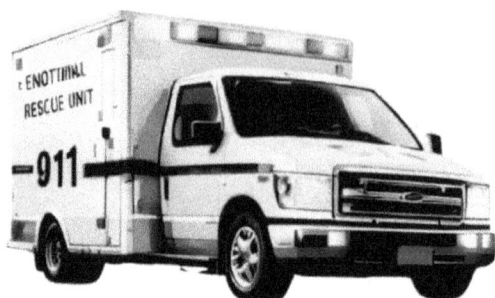

Big Sis Says

THE POINT OF
HEALING IS NOT TO
LOVE WHO HURT YOU

–

IT'S TO LOVE
YOURSELF ENOUGH
TO NEVER CHOOSE
THAT VERSION OF
LIFE AGAIN.

The Universe Slid Your Chair Back on Purpose…

"The Universe Slid Your Chair Back on Purpose…"

Let me tell you something that'll save you years of frustration, therapy bills, and emotional overdraft fees:

**The universe didn't delay you —
it positioned you.**

You thought you were being held up.
You thought you were being ignored.
You thought life was playing in your face.

But hear Big Sis clearly:

The universe slid your chair back so you could see the whole table.

Because you?
You were about to make a permanent decision
based on a temporary angle.

You were inches away from signing off on something
that wasn't the full picture.
You were close to settling, accepting, approving, or finalizing something
that wasn't the *blessing* —
it was the **practice round.**

Life said,
"Uh-uh,
Sit back.
Look again."

Delays are not denials – they are divine disruptions.

Sometimes God will tap you on the shoulder so gently you miss it.
Other times, He will spin your chair around
like,
"NO MA'AM — look at THIS."

When your chair slides back:

- You see the cracks you overlooked.
- You see the truth you weren't ready to admit.
- You see the opportunities you would've missed.
- You see the growth you didn't know you needed.

You see **the whole assignment**, not a cropped preview.

The truth? You weren't ready to see this blessing up close.

Not because you're lacking —
but because your **vision wasn't calibrated** yet.

You needed a pause.
You needed clarity.
You needed that extra insight.
You needed to clean up loose ends you didn't even know were dangling.

And…
look at what happened during that "delay":

You caught mistakes.
You added brilliance.
You deepened the message.
You refined the purpose.
You expanded the reach.
You transformed the entire project.

Ain't that wild?

You weren't behind schedule.
You were **synced with divine timing**.

Sometimes the universe slows you down so you don't shortchange yourself.

You were about to release a smaller version of your greatness.
A rushed version.
A half-cooked version.
A "good enough" version.

But you're not called to "good enough."
You're called to **impact**,
legacy,
transformation,
and **receipts**.

So your chair slid back so you could see:

- What you missed
- What you needed
- And what you deserved

And now?

Now you're building with the *full picture*, not a guess.

Now the book is richer.
The message is sharper.
The healing is deeper.
The purpose is louder.
The steps forward are cleaner.

You were never delayed.
You were being **prepared**.

Let this be your takeaway:

When your chair slides back, don't panic.
Don't pout.
Don't push forward.
Pause.
You're being given the luxury of clarity.
You're being allowed to see the whole table —
not just the plate in front of you.

And when you can see the whole table?

You make decisions like a woman who knows who she is.

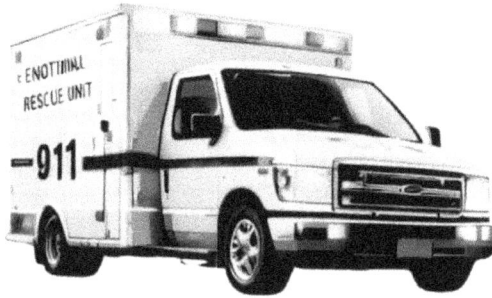

Big Sis Says

WHEN THE UNIVERSE
SLID YOUR CHAIR
BACK,
IT WASN'T REJECTION
– IT WAS DIRECTION.
YOU WERE TOO CLOSE
TO THE WRONG TABLE
TO RECOGNIZE YOUR
NEXT BLESSING.

A Word From The Community

"While the G.A.G. Method is very helpful in building self-awareness and confidence, the true strength of this program lies in its leaders. L.A. Walker and Dr. Marcia Norris demonstrate remarkable sensitivity to individual needs and concerns. I am deeply grateful for their guidance during a difficult season of my life."

Carolyn B. Yucha, RN, PhD
Professor and Dean Emeritus, School of Nursing, University of Nevada, Las Vegas, Editor, *Biological Research for Nursing*

The G.A.G. Method — Good, Amazing, And Great

The Chapter That Rebuilds You From the Inside Out

Before the heartbreak…
Before the betrayal…
Before the kitchen-floor breakdown while the toast burned and your hope burned with it…

There was a woman inside you who already knew who she was.

Life tried to make her forget.
The wrong relationships drained her.
The emotional freeloaders trained her to ignore herself.
The pressure bent her.
The silence smothered her.

But here's the secret the world didn't know:

You came into this life with a reset button.
A recalibration tool.
A comeback mechanism coded into your spirit.

It's called **The G.A.G. Method**:

GOOD. AMAZING. GREAT.

And let me be clear—this is not a cute phrase.
This is a spiritual defibrillator.
It brings you back to life when life tries to take you out.

This chapter is your reminder—
and your permission—
to rewrite the entire story of YOU.

1. GOOD — The Recognition Stage

Good is where you end free-falling and finally catch your breath.

Good is when you shun explaining, stop defending, wave goodbye to spiraling, and say:

"I am still GOOD... even if they mishandled me."

Good isn't perfection.
Good is clarity.

Good is when you tell the truth:

I'm hurting.
I'm grieving.
I'm disappointed.
I'm exhausted.

But I am **not** destroyed.

Good is the moment you whisper:

"I deserve better than this version of love."

Good is the woman who survived the storm.

2. AMAZING — The Rebuild

Amazing is where the magic starts tightening its shoes.

Amazing is the season when people who once knew you...
don't recognize you anymore.

Amazing is when you:

- Reinstate your boundaries.
- Take your voice off mute.

- You **no longer apologize** for wanting peace.
- You **no longer rescue** adults who refuse to grow.
- You **no longer shrink** so someone else can feel tall.

Amazing is when you look in the mirror and meet the woman grief thought it killed…

She survived it.
And she glows now.

Amazing sounds like this:

**"I am not here to be chosen.
I am here to choose."**

3. GREAT — The Graduation

Great is the evolution.
Great is the steady.
Great is the crown placed back on your own head—by YOU.

Great doesn't shout.
Great doesn't argue.
Great doesn't explain its price tag.

Great simply says:

"This time, I'm building a life that includes ME."

Great is when you no longer find value in:

- Settling
- Shrinking
- Dimming your light
- Explaining your worth
- Performing for crumbs

- Breaking yourself into pieces to fit small places

Great is when the chapter ends with:

"Bye Bitch. Bye."

And you walk toward the life that already had your name on it.

4. How G.A.G. Heals What Broke You

G.A.G. isn't a slogan.
G.A.G. is a healing architecture.

Every wound you've ever carried fits into one of these stages:

GOOD — You recognize what hurt you.
AMAZING — You reclaim what was stolen from you.
GREAT — You rise into who you were always meant to be.

If heartbreak was the demolition crew,
G.A.G. is the blueprint.

If betrayal was the fire,
G.A.G. is the rebuild.

If the "old you" died in the chaos,
G.A.G. is the resurrection.

Healing finally begins where it always belonged:

Inside you.

Not in the apology they'll never give.
Not in the closure they refused to provide.
Not in the truth they were afraid to tell.

Inside **YOU**.

5. The G.A.G. Moment

Every woman has a G.A.G. moment.

It's the second you realize:

"I'm not begging anymore."
"I'm not repeating myself."
"I'm not fixing what I didn't break."
"I'm not being someone's unpaid therapist."
"I'm not catching a case behind anybody."
"I'm done sacrificing myself for peace they never gave back."

That's the moment you inhale your power
and exhale the pain.

That moment becomes the first brick of your new life.

6. G.A.G. Is a Practice — Not a Performance

You do not have to be healed every day.
You do not have to be strong every moment.

Some days you'll feel **Great** — clear, confident, unbothered.
Some days you'll feel **Amazing** — hopeful, rebuilding, steady.
Some days you'll feel **Good enough to show up** — and that counts.

Healing is not a straight line.
It's a return path.

And the power of G.A.G. is this:
You don't start over when you have a bad day.
You don't "fail" healing because you cried, missed them, or felt triggered.
You simply check in and ask:

Where am I today — Good, Amazing, or Great?

Then you respond accordingly.

- On **Good** days, you rest, tell the truth, and protect your energy.
- On **Amazing** days, you reinforce boundaries and practice new choices.
- On **Great** days, you build, expand, and move forward without apology.

No shame.
No rushing.
No self-betrayal disguised as growth.

G.A.G. gives you permission to be human *and* intentional.

7. The Promise of the G.A.G. Method

Here's what G.A.G. guarantees — if you use it honestly:

You will stop romanticizing what hurt you.
You will stop negotiating with red flags.
You will stop confusing familiarity with safety.
You will stop calling survival "love."

And slowly — quietly — power returns.

Not the loud kind.
Not the prove-it kind.
The grounded kind.

The kind where:

- you don't chase clarity,
- you don't explain boundaries,
- you don't stay where you're diminished,
- and you don't abandon yourself to keep anyone.

That's Great energy.

Final Big Sis Word

You were never broken.
You were interrupted.

The G.A.G. Method doesn't turn you into someone new.
It brings you **back** to yourself —
with wisdom,
with scars,
with discernment,
and with your standards intact.

So when life asks again,
"How are you doing?"

You'll smile — not because everything is perfect,
but because you finally know the truth:

I'm Good.
I'm Amazing.
I'm Great. And this time — I know how to stay that way.

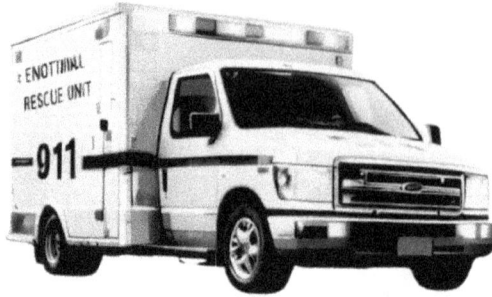

Big Sis Says

GOOD. AMAZING. GREAT.
STOP CELEBRATING
CRUMBS AND CALLING
IT A FEAST.
YOUR LIFE GETS BETTER
THE MOMENT YOU RAISE
YOUR STANDARD
AND KEEP IT THERE.

Big Sis Self-Check Assessment

Before you turn this page and walk into your new life,
Big Sis needs you to pause right here.

You cannot heal what you refuse to name.
You cannot reclaim what you never admitted you lost.
And you cannot step into your comeback story
carrying the same emotional luggage
that broke your heart the first time.

This is not a test —
it's a truth-telling moment.

Be honest.
Be gentle where you need softness.
Be honest where you need clarity.
And above all…
be real with yourself.

This is the page where your healing begins
and the excuses end.

Take your time.
Take your breath.
Take your power back.

Now let's reflect… and reclaim.

Reflect & Reclaim

1. What actually happened — not the softened version?

(Clarity is step one. Delusion is expensive.)

- A. I told myself a story that hurt less.
- B. I ignored what I saw because I didn't want the truth.
- C. I excused behavior I would've checked in a stranger.
- D. I minimized red flags because I wanted it to work.
- **E. Other:** _____

2. Which emotion did you feel first?

(Your first emotion tells the truth your mouth won't say.)

- A. Shock
- B. Anger
- C. Confusion
- D. A pain I can't describe
- **E. Other:** _____

3. How did you respond to the hurt?

(Patterns repeat until you replace them.)

- A. I shut down.
- B. I chased answers I already knew.
- C. I begged, bargained, or overexplained.
- D. I pretended I was fine.
- **E. Other:** _____

4. What lie did you tell yourself to survive the moment?

(We've all done it — don't judge the version of you that was hurting.)

- A. "It's not that bad."
- B. "They'll come around."
- C. "Maybe I deserved it."
- D. "I can fix this."

- **E. Other:** _____

5. What truth showed up later?

(Truth walks slow but hits hard.)

- A. I should've left earlier.
- B. They were never going to change.
- C. The love was one-sided.
- D. My spirit was tired long before my body left.
- **E. Other:** _____

6. What is one promise you can make to yourself right now?

(This is the contract for your comeback.)

- A. I will not ignore myself to keep someone else comfortable.
- B. I will honor my intuition the first time.
- **C.** I will choose environments that choose me back.
- **D.** I will detach from anything that drains me.
- **E.** I will love myself loudly.
- **F. Other:** _____

7. Who are you becoming as you heal?

(Name her. Become her.)

- A. Someone who no longer apologizes for existing.
- B. Someone who trusts her voice again.
- C. Someone who refuses half-love and half-effort.
- D. Someone who guards her peace like property.
- **E. Other:** _____

8. What boundary will protect the future you?

(A healed woman with boundaries is a whole security system.)

- A. No more second chances for first-time disrespect.
- B. If it confuses me, it loses me.
- C. I will not carry what is not mine.
- D. Silence is an answer — and I will listen.
- **E. Other:** _____

9. What part of you needs the most compassion right now?

(Hold her gently — she survived the explosion.)

- A. The version of me that loved too hard.
- B. The version that stayed too long.
- C. The version that didn't know better.
- D. The version learning to trust again.
- **E. Other:** _____

10. Which fear is trying to drag you backward?

(Fear lies. Intuition whispers.)

- A. Fear of being alone.
- B. Fear of starting over.
- C. Fear that this pain is permanent.
- D. Fear I'll choose wrong again.
- **E. Other:** _____

11. What truth are you finally ready to accept?

(Acceptance is the doorway to peace.)

- A. They were not my person.

- B. I deserved better the entire time.
- C. Leaving saved my spirit.
- D. My healing is my responsibility.
- **E. Other:** _____

12. What is your comeback declaration?

(This is your rebirth talking.)

- A. I am choosing myself without hesitation.
- B. I am letting go of what hurt me.
- C. I am rebuilding with wisdom, not wounds.
- D. I am ready for the version of me I've prayed for.
- **E. Other:** _____

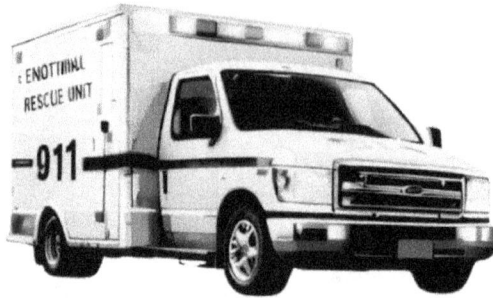

Big Sis Says

BEFORE YOU RISE,
ASK YOURSELF:
"AM I CHOOSING
FROM FEAR... OR
FROM SELF-RESPECT?"
YOUR ANSWER WILL
TELL YOU
EVERYTHING ABOUT
YOUR NEXT STEP.

SEGMENT III
CAN WE CHAT...

Real Conversations About Love, Power, and Choice

Naming What Happened

This part of the book isn't about stories.
It's about understanding.

About being able to say—maybe for the first time—
Here's what this was.
Here's why it hurts.
And here's why I wasn't crazy.

Many people arrive here still circling their feelings, unsure how to describe what they lived through. Not because they lack insight, but because the experience itself was disorienting. When reality keeps shifting, it's hard to trust your own perceptions—let alone articulate them.

This section exists to give language to what never had clarity while you were inside it.

There are no characters to follow here.
No scenes to replay.
No moments to dramatize.

Some experiences don't need a story to be real.
They need recognition.

These reflections are meant to help you name patterns, understand emotional injuries that didn't make sense at the time, and release the quiet self-blame that often lingers long after a relationship ends.

You're not being asked to reach conclusions.
You're being invited to see more clearly.

Take what resonates.
Leave what doesn't.

This is where understanding begins.

CAN WE CHAT?

Loving Someone Who Couldn't Tell the Truth

I didn't fall in love with a lie.
I fell in love with someone who made lying feel invisible.

That's the part people don't understand.

When you're not a liar, deception isn't your first conclusion. You assume misunderstanding. You assume fear. You assume timing. You assume there's a reason that will eventually make sense if you stay open long enough.

So you keep circling.

Things feel mostly fine—until they don't. Details don't quite line up, but they don't feel dangerous either. They feel incomplete. And instead of questioning them, you fill in the gaps with trust.

You don't accuse.
You adjust.

You tell yourself, *If something were really wrong, I'd know.*
But the truth doesn't arrive all at once. It comes in fragments.

That's what makes it so painful.

Because you're not reacting to one betrayal. You're slowly realizing that entire stretches of your life were built on information that wasn't real.

The hardest part isn't even the lies themselves.
It's the time.

The years spent explaining inconsistencies.
The emotional labor of making sense of stories that were never meant

to make sense.
The moments you defended someone, only to later realize you were defending fiction.

Truth has a way of insisting on being known.
It doesn't rush, but it doesn't disappear either.

Eventually, it steps forward—quietly but unmistakably—and you're left standing there with a realization that lands all at once:

I have been living inside something that wasn't true.

That's when the grief shows up.

Not just grief for the relationship, but for the version of yourself who kept believing clarity was one more conversation away. One more explanation. One more chance.

You weren't foolish.
You weren't naïve.
You weren't ignoring reality.

You were loving from a place that assumed truth mattered to both of you.

And when honesty isn't mutual, love doesn't fail because you didn't try hard enough.
It fails because the ground underneath it was never solid.

Big Sis Commentary: How This Happens — And What It Does

This kind of relationship doesn't fall apart all at once.
It erodes slowly.

It happens because you're operating from good faith while someone else is operating from concealment. You're trying to understand. They're trying to manage perception.

So the relationship becomes a loop.

You sense something is off.
They offer an explanation.
You accept it — not because it fully satisfies you, but because you want peace more than confrontation.

Over time, that adjustment becomes a habit.

You start carrying the responsibility for clarity.
You become the one who remembers, explains, reconciles, and smooths over inconsistencies. Not because you're weak — but because you're relational.

What this does to you is subtle but profound.

You begin doubting your instincts.
You over-contextualize behavior that doesn't make sense.
You stay longer because nothing is *provably* wrong — even though something is deeply untrue.

And here's what this kind of relationship should **never** be doing:

It should not require you to suspend reality to stay connected.
It should not make you responsible for holding the story together.
It should not ask you to keep believing when the truth keeps slipping.

If you're exhausted not from conflict, but from *trying to understand*, that's information.

And if clarity only arrives after years of circling, it doesn't mean you failed.

It means the truth was never being shared — only managed.

No diagnosis.
No shame.
Just clarity.

CAN WE CHAT?

Sex Addiction vs. Love… and Love Addiction vs. Love

SECTION 1 — Let's Stop Calling Everything "Love"

Can we chat?

Because we use the word *love* to explain a lot of things that are actually compulsion, avoidance, or emotional survival strategies.

Sex addiction isn't love.
Love addiction isn't love.

But they *feel* like love when you don't know what you're looking at.

And that confusion is where people get hurt — quietly, repeatedly, and with a lot of self-blame.

COMMENTARY

Intensity is not intimacy.
Attachment is not connection.

And chemistry without clarity
is how people confuse chaos for romance.

SECTION 2 — What Sex Addiction Actually Is

Sex addiction isn't about sex.
It's about regulation.

Sex addiction looks like:

- Compulsive sexual behavior
- Escalation over time

- Risk without regard for consequences
- Emotional numbing through sexual stimulation
- Using sex to avoid discomfort, stress, or self-awareness

In plain Big Sis language:
Sex becomes a coping mechanism — not a connection.

The person isn't chasing *you*.
They're chasing relief.

And relief doesn't bond.
It consumes.

COMMENTARY

Sex addiction doesn't deepen intimacy.
It bypasses it.

And no amount of loyalty
can compete with a compulsion.

SECTION 3 — Love Addiction Is Not Romantic

Now let's talk about the one that gets praised.

Love addiction doesn't look reckless.
It looks devoted.
Patient.
Understanding.

Love addiction sounds like:

- "If I just love them better…"
- "They're wounded — I can help."
- "Leaving feels worse than staying."
- "I'll abandon myself before I abandon them."

Love addiction isn't about loving someone.
It's about needing someone to feel okay.

The relationship becomes the oxygen.

COMMENTARY

Love addiction disguises itself as loyalty.
But loyalty that costs you your identity
isn't noble.

It's dangerous.

SECTION 4 — What Real Love Actually Requires

Love isn't urgent.
It isn't frantic.
It doesn't ask you to disappear.

Real love includes:

- Mutual regulation
- Choice, not compulsion
- Desire with restraint
- Connection without control
- Safety in disagreement

Love doesn't need you to earn it through endurance.
It doesn't punish boundaries.
It doesn't escalate chaos to feel alive.

If love feels like survival —
something else is happening.

COMMENTARY

Love expands your nervous system.
Addiction hijacks it.

And the body always knows the difference
before the mind does.

SECTION 5 — Why People Confuse Them

Because sex addiction feels exciting.
Because love addiction feels meaningful.
Because both create intensity.

And intensity feels like purpose
when you're starving for connection.

But love doesn't drain you to prove itself.
It doesn't keep you anxious, guessing, or depleted.

If the relationship only feels good
when you're chasing, rescuing, or sacrificing —
That's not love. That's a cycle.

COMMENTARY — Big Sis Says

Sex addiction uses bodies.
Love addiction abandons self.
Love requires presence.

You don't heal addiction by loving harder.
You heal it by stepping out of the pattern.

Besides…
If it feels intoxicating but unsafe,
urgent but unstable,
deep but draining —

that's not love. That's a warning.

CAN WE CHAT?

Narcissism: The Word, the Traits, and the Web

SECTION 1 — Let's Clear The Room

Can we chat for a minute?
Because *narcissist* has become the new *toxic* —
overused, under-understood, and thrown at anyone who hurts our
feelings and doesn't apologize fast enough.

Not everyone who disappoints you is a narcissist.
Not everyone who leaves you is a narcissist.
Not everyone who's selfish, avoidant, emotionally immature, or bad at
love qualifies.

Sometimes people are just… not your people.

And sometimes —
they really are dangerous to your nervous system.

Clarity starts with knowing the difference.

COMMENTARY

Mislabeling pain doesn't heal it.
Understanding patterns does.

Calling everyone a narcissist
keeps you stuck in reaction
instead of moving you toward protection.

SECTION 2 — What Narcissism Actually Is

True narcissism is not confidence.
It's not self-love.
It's not ambition.

Narcissism is a **relational disorder** rooted in fragile identity.

At its core, narcissism looks like this:

- A deep need for validation
- A lack of empathy when it conflicts with their needs
- A pattern of control, not connection
- An inability to tolerate accountability
- A reliance on external supply to regulate self-worth

In plain Big Sis language:
They don't *relate* to people.
They *use* people to stabilize themselves.

And when you stop serving that purpose —
they destabilize *you*.

COMMENTARY

Narcissists don't destroy relationships accidentally.
They destabilize them strategically.

Not because they're evil —
but because self-reflection feels like annihilation.

SECTION 3 — Narcissistic Traits Vs. Narcissism

Now listen carefully — this part matters.

You can have **narcissistic traits**
without being a narcissist.

Traits include:

- Defensiveness
- Avoidance
- Ego protection
- Insecurity masked as arrogance
- Difficulty apologizing

Most humans display these under stress.

Narcissism, however, is a *pattern* — not a phase.

If the behavior:

- repeats
- escalates
- punishes boundaries
- rewrites reality
- erodes your self-trust

You're not dealing with a bad moment.
You're dealing with a system.

And systems don't change because you love harder.

COMMENTARY

Traits can be worked on.
Patterns require protection.

Knowing the difference
can save you years of explaining yourself
to someone committed to misunderstanding you.

SECTION 4 — The Web People Don't See

Here's where most people get caught.

Narcissists don't lure you with cruelty.
They lure you with *connection*.

They mirror you.
Validate you.
Accelerate intimacy.
Create a sense of "finally."

And once you're bonded,
the rules change.

Confusion replaces clarity.
You start doubting your memory.
You over-explain normal needs.
You carry emotional weight that isn't yours.

This is the web.

And the web tightens when you don't know it exists.

COMMENTARY

You don't fall for narcissists because you're weak.
You fall because you're empathetic, hopeful, and relational.

The trap isn't love.
The trap is unarmed love.

SECTION 5 — Arming Yourself With Knowledge

Knowledge doesn't make you cynical.
It makes you selective.

When you understand narcissism, you stop asking:
"What did I do wrong?"

And start asking:
"What pattern am I in?"

You learn to watch behavior — not words.
You trust your body — not their explanations.
You stop negotiating your reality for temporary peace.

This isn't about labeling people.
It's about **protecting your nervous system**.

Because the most dangerous relationships
aren't loud.

They're confusing.

COMMENTARY — Big Sis Says

Understanding narcissism isn't about revenge.
It's about recognition.

You don't need a diagnosis to walk away from damage.
You need clarity.

And clarity is how you stop repeating the lesson
with a different face.

Besides…
If love requires you to abandon yourself,
that's not romance.

That's entanglement.

CAN WE CHAT...

Why Strong Women Stay Too Long

SECTION 1 — Strength Gets Misread

Strong women don't stay because they're weak.
They stay because they're capable.

They've survived hard things before.
They've adapted.
They've carried weight without collapsing.

So when a relationship becomes difficult,
they don't panic —
they problem-solve.

They ask better questions.
They offer grace.
They assume responsibility.

And that's where the trap opens.

COMMENTARY

Strength without discernment
turns endurance into a liability.

What you can survive
is not always what you should.

SECTION 2 — Confidence Becomes A Challenge

Strong women are used to figuring things out.

So when love doesn't work easily,
it feels like a puzzle — not a warning.

They think:

- "I just haven't cracked this yet."
- "I've handled worse."
- "Growth is uncomfortable."

And sometimes that's true.

But sometimes the relationship isn't challenging you —
it's consuming you.

COMMENTARY

A challenge grows you.
A drain shrinks you.

Knowing the difference
is a form of wisdom.

SECTION 3 — Loyalty Gets Weaponized

Strong women value loyalty.
They don't quit quickly.
They don't abandon at the first sign of struggle.

So when a relationship starts hurting,
they double down.

They stay when clarity says go.
They explain when silence is loud.
They empathize past the point of self-protection.

Not because they're naïve —
but because they're principled.

COMMENTARY

Loyalty without reciprocity
is self-sacrifice in a nicer outfit.

SECTION 4 — Strength Becomes A Cover

Here's the quiet truth:

Strong women are often chosen
by people who don't want equals.

They want stability.
They want tolerance.
They want someone who can *handle them*.

And strength becomes permission
to offer less.

"You're strong — you'll be fine."
"You understand me."
"You don't need as much."

Until strong starts feeling lonely.

COMMENTARY

Being strong doesn't mean
you need less love.

It means you deserve consistency — not excuses.

SECTION 5 — The Turning Point

Strong women leave late
because they leave *clean*.

They don't leave on impulse.
They leave after clarity.

After trying.
After adjusting.
After knowing — without doubt —
that staying costs more than going.

And when they leave,
it's not dramatic.

It's decisive.

COMMENTARY — Big Sis Says

Strong women don't stay too long
because they don't know better.

They stay because they believe effort matters.

But love isn't proven by endurance.
It's proven by care.

Besides…
If your strength is being used against you,
It's time to go where you don't have to be strong to be loved.

CAN WE CHAT…

Because Love Was Oversold

SECTION 1 — The Promise We Were Sold

Love was marketed as the solution.

If you love hard enough,
wait long enough,
try again,
communicate better,
heal more —

everything will work out.

Love was positioned as the glue, the fix, the reward, and the proof.

And so we believed:
If it hurts, love more.
If it's confusing, love deeper.
If it's draining, love harder.

Nobody told us love was never meant to carry everything by itself.

COMMENTARY

Love is powerful —
but it is not structural support.

You can't build stability
on feelings alone.

SECTION 2 — What Love Can Actually Do

Love can create connection.
Love can inspire care.
Love can motivate growth.

Love can soften hard moments.
Love can deepen intimacy.

But love **cannot**:

- regulate another person
- replace accountability
- correct incompatibility
- heal untreated trauma
- override misalignment

When love is asked to do these jobs,
it collapses under the weight.

COMMENTARY

Love is not supposed to fix people.
It's supposed to *meet* them.

Anything else is projection.

SECTION 3 — Where We Got Misled

We were taught love is enough.

But love without:

- boundaries
- communication
- shared values

- emotional safety
- responsibility

becomes endurance — not partnership.

This is how people stay too long.
This is how effort replaces joy.
This is how pain gets reframed as growth.

Love wasn't failing.
It was being misused.

COMMENTARY

If love requires constant self-abandonment,
it's not devotion. It's depletion.

SECTION 4 — What Actually Makes Relationships Work

Healthy relationships run on more than love.

They require:

- mutual regulation
- emotional literacy
- repair after conflict
- aligned life direction
- respect that doesn't disappear under stress

Love adds warmth.
These provide structure.

Without structure,
love leaks everywhere.

COMMENTARY

Love is the spark.
Compatibility is the engine.

One without the other
doesn't get you far.

SECTION 5 — The Reframe That Frees People

When love is oversold,
People blame themselves when relationships fail.

They think:
"I didn't love enough."
"I quit too soon."
"I should've tried harder."

But sometimes the truth is simpler:

Love showed up.
The rest didn't.

And that doesn't make you heartless.
It makes you honest.

COMMENTARY — Big Sis Says

Love is not supposed to hurt this much.
It's supposed to be supported.

You don't fail at love
because something ends.

You fail when you stay
where love is doing all the work alone.

Besides…
Love was never meant to be the whole system.

It's just one part.

CAN WE CHAT...
Compatibility Isn't Romantic — It's Essential

SECTION 1 — Why Compatibility Gets Ignored

Compatibility doesn't sell well.

It doesn't sparkle.
It doesn't rush your pulse.
It doesn't feel cinematic.

Compatibility sounds practical.
Unsexy.
Almost boring.

So we're taught to prioritize chemistry, passion, and intensity —
and treat compatibility like a bonus feature instead of a requirement.

But chemistry gets you interested.
Compatibility determines whether you can stay.

COMMENTARY

Chemistry opens the door.
Compatibility decides whether the house is livable.

One excites you.
The other sustains you.

SECTION 2 — What Compatibility Actually Is

Compatibility isn't having everything in common.
It's having **alignment where it matters**.

Compatibility looks like:

- similar emotional needs
- comparable communication styles
- aligned values around money, time, and responsibility
- conflict that can be repaired
- nervous systems that don't constantly clash

It's not about sameness.
It's about *fit*.

Love can exist without compatibility —
but peace cannot.

COMMENTARY

Love feels good at first.
Incompatibility feels expensive later.

And the bill always comes due.

SECTION 3 — Why Love Can't Override It

This is where people get stuck.

They say:
"But we love each other."

Love doesn't make misalignment disappear.
It just makes you tolerate it longer.

You can love someone deeply
and still feel chronically misunderstood, exhausted, or unseen.

That doesn't mean love failed.
It means compatibility was missing.

COMMENTARY

Love without compatibility
turns into management.

And nobody wants to manage
their own relationship.

SECTION 4 — How Incompatibility Shows Up

Incompatibility rarely announces itself loudly.

It shows up as:

- constant compromise by the same person
- recurring arguments with no resolution
- feeling lonely while partnered
- emotional translation fatigue
- one person shrinking to keep things working

You don't feel unsafe —
you feel tired.

That's not normal relationship stress.
That's misalignment.

COMMENTARY

If love requires you to work this hard
just to feel okay,
something fundamental is off.

SECTION 5 — Why Compatibility Is Actually Romantic

Compatibility is waking up without dread.
It's being understood without a speech.
It's conflict that ends in repair — not distance.

Compatibility creates:

- ease
- trust
- mutual effort
- emotional rest

That *is* romance —
just not the dramatic kind.

COMMENTARY — Big Sis Says

Compatibility isn't boring.
It's peaceful.

And peace doesn't give you butterflies —
It gives you longevity.

Besides…
Love makes you want to stay.
Compatibility makes it possible.

CAN WE CHAT...

Why "Just Do It Anyway" Backfires

SECTION 1 — The Advice We Were Given

"Just do it anyway."

Have sex anyway.
Show up anyway.
Stay anyway.
Try anyway.

We were taught that effort fixes distance.
That pushing through discomfort proves commitment.
That desire will follow action if you're disciplined enough.

So people override their bodies,
silence their intuition,
and perform connection instead of addressing disconnection.

And for a while, it seems like it works.

Until it doesn't.

COMMENTARY

Effort without alignment
doesn't build intimacy.

It builds resentment.

SECTION 2 — What "Anyway" Really Means

"Just do it anyway" usually translates to:

182

Ignore your discomfort.
Suppress your truth.
Delay the conversation.

It teaches people to override themselves
instead of listening inward.

But the body keeps score.

Every forced yes,
every swallowed no,
every moment you show up against yourself
gets stored.

And stored resentment doesn't dissolve on its own.

COMMENTARY

You can override your nervous system —
but it will remember.

And it always collects later.

SECTION 3 — Why It Kills Desire

Desire requires choice.
Safety.
Presence.

When intimacy becomes something you *push through*,
your body stops offering it freely.

You may still participate —
but you're no longer engaged.

That's not passion fading.
That's self-protection activating.

COMMENTARY

Desire doesn't disappear.
It withdraws.

Usually to protect you
from further emotional debt.

SECTION 4 — The Long-Term Damage

"Just do it anyway" creates short-term peace
and long-term distance.

People stay longer than they should.
They avoid necessary conversations.
They confuse endurance with maturity.

And eventually, intimacy feels transactional.
Connection feels forced.
Love feels heavy.

Not because love failed —
but because honesty was postponed.

COMMENTARY

Avoidance always charges interest.

And the longer you delay truth,
the higher the cost.

SECTION 5 — What Actually Works

Real repair doesn't come from pushing through.

It comes from pausing.

Naming what's off.
Restoring safety.
Rebalancing effort.
Allowing desire to return organically.

Doing less *anyway*
creates more space for real connection.

COMMENTARY — Big Sis Says

"Just do it anyway" teaches people
to betray themselves quietly.

And self-betrayal always backfires —
in intimacy, trust, and self-respect.

Besides…
If you have to force closeness,
it's already time to talk or walk.

CAN WE CHAT...
What Support Actually Looks Like (When Money Shifts)

SECTION 1 — When The Numbers Change

Support gets romanticized.

People imagine it looks like endless patience,
quiet sacrifice,
and saying "we'll figure it out" without flinching.

But when finances shift, support gets practical fast.

Money stress doesn't whisper.
It interrupts sleep.
It changes tone.
It tightens everything.

A diagnosis, job loss, or reduced capacity doesn't just affect income —
it rearranges power, fear, and decision-making.

COMMENTARY

Money doesn't create tension.
It reveals it.

SECTION 2 — What Support Is Not

Support is not pretending you're fine when you're not.
It's not absorbing stress silently.
It's not taking on everything without conversation.

Support does **not** mean:

- ignoring your own anxiety
- downplaying financial fear
- becoming the sole stabilizer without consent
- pretending love cancels math

Martyrdom is not support.
It's avoidance dressed up as loyalty.

COMMENTARY

If support requires silence,
it isn't support — it's suppression.

SECTION 3 — What Support Actually Requires

Real support during financial strain looks like transparency.

Honest numbers.
Shared decision-making.
Revised expectations.

It sounds like:

- "This scares me too."
- "We need to adjust together."
- "I can help, but I have limits."
- "Let's talk before resentment sets in."

Support is collaborative —
not heroic.

COMMENTARY

Support works best
when no one is secretly drowning.

SECTION 4 — The Shift In Identity

Financial change can trigger shame —
especially for the partner whose income dropped.

Support isn't rescuing someone from that shame.
It's refusing to weaponize it.

It means separating worth from productivity.
It means protecting dignity alongside practicality.

And it also means allowing the supporting partner
to feel the weight — without guilt.

COMMENTARY

You can protect someone's dignity
without carrying the entire load alone.

SECTION 5 — When Support Needs Structure

Support lasts longer with structure.

Budgets.
Boundaries.
Timelines.
Outside help when needed.

Love doesn't require unlimited capacity.
It requires sustainability.

And sustainability demands honesty —
especially about money.

COMMENTARY — Big Sis Says

Support isn't saying "I'll handle it" until you burn out.

It's saying,
"Let's face this together — realistically."

Besides...
Love can survive a financial shift.
Resentment can't.

And support that costs you your stability
will eventually cost the relationship.

CAN WE CHAT...

When Love Meets a Diagnosis

SECTION 1 — When Life Interrupts the Plan

No one plans for illness.

It arrives uninvited,
unchoreographed,
and immediately rewrites the relationship contract.

One appointment.
One scan.
One sentence you can't unhear.

And suddenly love isn't just about compatibility, laughter, or shared dreams —
it's about doctors, medications, uncertainty, and fear you don't know how to name yet.

You don't stop loving your partner.
But love changes shape.

COMMENTARY

A diagnosis doesn't just affect the body.
It enters the relationship.

And pretending otherwise helps no one.

SECTION 2 — What Love Feels Like After the News

Love becomes quieter.

Not weaker — quieter.

It shows up as vigilance.
As research tabs open at 2 a.m.
As watching for pain without staring.
As pretending you're okay when you're not, because you don't want to add weight to an already heavy moment.

The partner receiving the diagnosis is grieving their body, their future, their identity.

The partner loving them is grieving too —
often in silence.

COMMENTARY

Caregivers grieve while still showing up.

And that grief deserves language.

SECTION 3 — The Myth Of "Be Strong"

People will tell you to be strong.
To stay positive.
To focus on gratitude.

But strength without honesty becomes isolation.

You are allowed to feel afraid.
You are allowed to feel overwhelmed.
You are allowed to miss the ease you had before.

Loving someone through illness doesn't require you to disappear.

COMMENTARY

Love isn't proven by suffering quietly.
It's sustained by truth.

SECTION 4 — When Care and Identity Shift

This is the part no one prepares you for.

Roles change.
Energy shifts.
Intimacy recalibrates.

You may become a supporter, an advocate, a scheduler, a protector.

And if you're not careful,
you stop being a partner.

That doesn't mean you're failing.
It means the relationship needs conscious tending —
not silent sacrifice.

COMMENTARY

Love should stretch —
not erase the person doing the loving.

SECTION 5 — What Makes Love Last Here

What sustains love through diagnosis isn't heroics.

It's communication.
Boundaries.
Shared honesty about limits.
Permission to rest.
Room for both people's emotions to exist without competition.

Love survives illness when both people are still allowed to be human.

COMMENTARY — Big Sis Says

Loving someone with a diagnosis doesn't mean pretending you're unbreakable.

It means choosing presence **with truth,**
care **with boundaries,**
and love **without self-erasure.**

Besides…
You can be devoted **and** honest.
Supportive **and** human.
And loving someone through illness should never cost you your own health.

If you want, the natural follow-ups to this topic could be:

- Caregiving vs. Codependency
- When Love Turns Into Management
- Staying Without Losing Yourself
- What Support Actually Looks Like
- When Walking Is Still Love

Just say the word.

What support actually looks like. I would like this to express when money is tight or finances have shifted

Here is the **complete Can We Chat conversation**, same format, with the financial reality centered and handled with dignity.

CAN WE CHAT...

Money, Power, and Unspoken Resentment

SECTION 1 — Where Power Quietly Shifts

Money doesn't just pay bills.
It sets the tone.

When one partner starts carrying more financially — whether suddenly or slowly — the balance in the relationship shifts.

Not always visibly.
But emotionally.

Decisions feel heavier.
Opinions carry different weight.
Silence grows around spending, saving, and security.

No one names it —
but everyone feels it.

COMMENTARY

Power doesn't announce itself.
It seeps.

SECTION 2 — How Resentment Takes Root

Resentment rarely starts as anger.

It starts as:

- unspoken pressure
- quiet scorekeeping

- delayed conversations
- "I'll handle it" said too many times

The supporting partner feels responsible.
The dependent partner feels watched.

Both feel tense.
Neither feels safe enough to say why.

And resentment grows best in silence.

COMMENTARY

What goes unsaid
doesn't disappear.

It compounds.

SECTION 3 — The Shame–Control Loop

When money shifts, shame often enters the room.

The partner earning less may feel:

- guilt
- inadequacy
- fear of being a burden

The partner earning more may feel:

- pressure
- authority they didn't ask for
- resentment they don't want

That combination creates a loop:
Shame on one side.
Control on the other.

Neither feels good.
Both damage intimacy.

COMMENTARY

Control often grows
where fear goes unspoken.

SECTION 4 — How Resentment Shows Up

Resentment doesn't always look like fights.

It looks like:

- passive comments
- delayed purchases being judged
- emotional withdrawal
- "must be nice" energy
- intimacy cooling without explanation

By the time resentment is obvious,
it's already been living there for a while.

COMMENTARY

Resentment is rarely about money.

It's about power without conversation.

SECTION 5 — What Actually Prevents It

Resentment dissolves in transparency.

Name the shift.
Discuss the fear.

Define limits early.
Revisit agreements often.

Power doesn't have to corrupt a relationship —
but pretending it isn't there will.

Shared clarity protects love better than silent sacrifice.

COMMENTARY — Big Sis Says

Money changes dynamics.
That's not failure — it's reality.

Resentment grows when power is felt
but never discussed.

Besides…
If one person holds the wallet
and the other holds the shame,
the relationship will eventually bleed.

Talk early.
Talk honestly.
Or resentment will do the talking for you.

CAN WE CHAT...

Accepting the Relationship Is Over

SECTION 1 — When You Already Know

Acceptance rarely arrives all at once.

It shows up in fragments.

In the way conversations feel forced.
In how silence feels heavier than words.
In the relief you feel when plans get canceled.

You keep telling yourself it's a phase.
Stress. Timing. Fatigue.

But deep down, you already know —
the relationship isn't alive anymore.

You're just maintaining it.

COMMENTARY

Knowing doesn't always feel dramatic.
Sometimes it just feels tired.

SECTION 2 — Why Acceptance Takes So Long

People don't stay because they're confused.
They stay because they're attached to meaning.

Shared history.
Inside jokes.
Versions of each other that no longer exist.

Letting go feels like erasing proof that love once mattered.

So you negotiate with reality.
You lower expectations.
You try one more conversation.

Not because you believe it will change —
but because ending it feels final.

COMMENTARY

Hope doesn't always mean belief.
Sometimes it just means delay.

SECTION 3 — The Grief That Comes First

Before acceptance comes grief.

Not just for the relationship —
but for the future you imagined.

The trips you won't take.
The routines you won't share.
The version of yourself that stayed longer than you should have.

Grief doesn't mean you made the wrong choice.
It means you cared.

COMMENTARY

Grief isn't weakness.
It's evidence of investment.

SECTION 4 — The Moment Acceptance Lands

Acceptance is quiet.

It's the moment you stop explaining.
Stop rehearsing arguments.
Stop waiting for closure that isn't coming.

You don't feel angry anymore.
You feel clear.

And clarity doesn't ask permission.

COMMENTARY

Closure isn't something you're given.
It's something you claim.

SECTION 5 — What Acceptance Actually Is

Acceptance isn't pretending it didn't hurt.
It's refusing to keep hurting yourself.

It's choosing peace over possibility.
Truth over endurance.
Self-respect over nostalgia.

You don't need a villain to leave.
You don't need betrayal to justify the ending.

Sometimes the relationship is over
because it already ended emotionally.

COMMENTARY — Big Sis Says

Accepting it's over doesn't mean love failed.

It means you stopped negotiating with reality.

Besides…
Staying after clarity isn't loyalty —
it's avoidance.

And walking away isn't giving up.
It's finally listening.

CAN WE CHAT...

How to Leave Without Burning Yourself Down

SECTION 1 — Why People Burn It All Down

Most people don't leave badly because they want chaos.
They leave badly because they're overwhelmed.

They're exhausted.
Unheard.
Carrying resentment they never learned how to name.

So when the decision finally comes,
everything spills at once.

Old arguments resurface.
Receipts come out.
Tone gets sharp.
Words get reckless.

Not because the relationship deserved destruction —
but because the exit was delayed too long.

COMMENTARY

Burning bridges often happens
when leaving was postponed past clarity.

SECTION 2 — What A Clean Exit Actually Requires

A clean exit starts *before* the goodbye

It requires internal alignment.

Knowing why you're leaving — without needing the other person to agree.
Letting go of the urge to be understood perfectly.
Accepting that discomfort is part of endings.

You don't need to convince someone.
You need to be consistent.

COMMENTARY

Peace doesn't come from winning the breakup.
It comes from ending it honestly.

SECTION 3 — Say Less, Mean More

People think closure comes from explanation.

It rarely does.

The more you explain,
the more you invite debate, bargaining, and distortion.

Clarity doesn't require a monologue.

"I'm done."
"This no longer works for me."
"I'm choosing to leave."

That's not cold.
That's contained.

COMMENTARY

Boundaries don't need speeches.
They need follow-through.

SECTION 4 — Resist The Urge To Prove Yourself

After you leave, there will be temptation.

To defend your choice.
To correct the narrative.
To respond to every message.

But self-respect grows in restraint.

You don't owe everyone access to your healing process.

Silence, used wisely, is not avoidance —
it's protection.

COMMENTARY

You don't have to attend every argument you're invited to.

SECTION 5 — What Leaving Well Really Looks Like

Leaving without burning yourself down means:

- No revenge tours
- No emotional dumping
- No rewriting history to justify the exit
- No self-betrayal for closure

It means walking away with your dignity intact.

You may still grieve.
You may still miss them.

But you won't have to heal from how you left.

COMMENTARY — Big Sis Says

Leaving well is an act of self-respect.

You don't have to scorch the earth
to prove the fire was real.

Besides…
If you leave with clarity,
you won't need ashes to remind you why you walked away.

CAN WE CHAT...
Why Re-Entering a Burning Building Is Risky

SECTION 1 — Why People Go Back

People don't go back because they forgot why they left.
They go back because the fire isn't burning *them* anymore — from a distance.

Time softens memory.
Loneliness edits reality.
Nostalgia highlights the good and crops out the danger.

And suddenly the smoke doesn't feel so thick.

So you tell yourself:
"Maybe it wasn't that bad."
"Maybe I overreacted."
"Maybe I can handle it now."

That's not growth talking.
That's familiarity calling.

COMMENTARY

Distance makes danger look manageable.

It isn't.

SECTION 2 — The Fire Never Asked You To Learn

Here's the truth people skip past:

The building didn't burn because you didn't try hard enough.
It burned because something was structurally wrong.

Unaddressed patterns don't heal during separation.
They wait.

You may have changed.
You may have learned.
You may have strengthened your boundaries.

But if the source of the fire hasn't changed,
re-entry is not reconciliation — it's exposure.

COMMENTARY

Healing doesn't make unsafe places safe.

It just makes you wiser about leaving them.

SECTION 3 — Why "This Time Will Be Different" Is Dangerous

Hope is powerful.
But hope without evidence is a liability.

People mistake emotional familiarity for emotional safety.
They confuse intensity with intimacy.
They interpret longing as a sign to return.

But wanting something doesn't mean it's good for you.

The fire doesn't care how much you missed the warmth.

COMMENTARY

What hurt you once
will hurt you again
if nothing changed but your tolerance.

SECTION 4 — The Cost of Going Back

Re-entering costs more than leaving did.

It costs credibility — with yourself.
It costs momentum — in your healing.
It costs clarity — because you start doubting your original decision.

And worst of all,
it teaches your nervous system that escape is temporary.

That's how cycles form.

COMMENTARY

Every return trains the body to stay longer next time.

SECTION 5 — What Safety Actually Looks Like

Safety doesn't require courage.
It requires consistency.

It looks like staying out once you leave.
Trusting the version of you who made the hard call.
Choosing peace over familiarity.

You don't need to prove you're stronger now
by walking back into what already hurt you.

COMMENTARY — Big Sis Says

If you had to evacuate,
It wasn't a misunderstanding.

Besides…
You don't re-enter a burning building
just because you miss the furniture.

Some exits are permanent
because survival depends on it.

CAN WE CHAT…
Don't Rush New Love — But Don't Deny It Either

SECTION 1 — THE OVERCORRECTION PHASE

After heartbreak, people swing hard.

Either they rush into something new
to prove they're still desirable, still chosen, still okay…

Or they lock love out completely,
mistaking isolation for healing
and avoidance for wisdom.

"I'm not ready."
"I need to work on myself."
"I can't trust anyone right now."

Sometimes that's true.
Sometimes it's fear wearing therapy language.

COMMENTARY

Healing isn't about closing your heart.
It's about reopening it with discernment.

SECTION 2 — Why Rushing Backfires

Rushing new love skips the integration phase.

You haven't processed the patterns yet.
You haven't recalibrated your boundaries.
You haven't fully heard what the last relationship taught you.

So you recreate familiarity instead of choosing differently.

New face.
Same dynamic.

That's not romance.
That's repetition.

COMMENTARY

Unhealed lessons
don't wait politely.

They reappear.

SECTION 3 — Why Denying Love Backfires Too

On the other side, denying love completely has its own cost.

You start seeing connection as a threat.
Interest feels intrusive.
Affection feels suspicious.

You confuse peace with numbness
and independence with emotional shutdown.

Healing doesn't require emotional starvation.

Love isn't the enemy.
Lack of awareness is.

COMMENTARY

You don't protect yourself
by becoming unavailable to life.

SECTION 4 — What Healthy Timing Actually Looks Like

Healthy timing isn't about calendars.

It's about capacity.

Can you stay present without losing yourself?
Can you enjoy connection without performing or panicking?
Can you say no without guilt — and yes without fear?

When the answer is mostly yes,
you're not rushing.

You're ready enough.

COMMENTARY

Readiness isn't certainty.
It's stability.

SECTION 5 — How To Hold New Love Correctly

You don't sprint.
You don't slam the brakes.

You walk.

You let things unfold without scripting the ending.
You stay curious instead of attached.
You allow joy without assigning forever.

New love doesn't need pressure.
It needs space.

COMMENTARY — Big Sis Says

You don't have to chase love —
and you don't have to hide from it either.

Besides…
If love shows up while you're healing,
you're allowed to say hello
without moving in.

Slow doesn't mean scared.
And open doesn't mean reckless.

CAN WE CHAT...
Letting Love Be Optional, Not Urgent

SECTION 1 — When Love Feels Like A Deadline

Somewhere along the way, love became urgent.

A timeline.
A fix.
A solution to loneliness, aging, fear, or unfinished dreams.

So people rush connections.
Force chemistry.
Over-invest early.

Not because the person is right —
but because being alone feels wrong.

Urgency doesn't come from desire.
It comes from pressure.

COMMENTARY

Love chosen in panic
rarely chooses you back.

SECTION 2 — Why Urgency Distorts Judgment

Urgency makes red flags look negotiable.
It turns incompatibility into "we can work on it."
It confuses attention with alignment.

When love feels urgent,
people tolerate confusion instead of seeking clarity.

Not because they're weak —
but because urgency shuts down discernment.

COMMENTARY

Nothing clouds judgment faster
than fear of being without.

SECTION 3 — What It Means To Make Love Optional

Optional doesn't mean indifferent.
It means unattached to the outcome.

You enjoy connection without assigning destiny.
You explore interest without abandoning standards.
You allow affection without surrendering your center.

Love becomes something you *choose* —
not something you *need to secure.*

COMMENTARY

Optional love is powerful
because it's voluntary.

SECTION 4 — How Optional Love Feels In The Body

There's no rush to prove.
No anxiety about where it's going.
No overthinking every interaction.

You're curious, not consumed.
Present, not performing.

And if it ends,
you grieve — but you don't collapse.

That's not detachment.
That's regulation.

COMMENTARY

Peace is the absence of urgency.

SECTION 5 — Why This Changes Everything

When love is optional,
you stop bargaining with yourself.

You don't stay to be chosen.
You don't chase to feel worthy.
You don't settle to feel safe.

You let love add to your life —
not define it.

COMMENTARY — BIG SIS SAYS

Love doesn't need urgency to be real.

Besides…
When love is optional,
you don't grab at it —
you recognize it.

And anything that needs to be rushed
probably isn't meant to last.

To Know You Is to Love You

(And Sometimes, to Fall in Love With You)

SECTION 1 — The Shift That Matters Most

There comes a point when love stops being about finding someone and starts being about finally seeing yourself.

Not the version shaped by survival.
Not the version that over-gives, over-explains, or over-stays.
But the version that knows when something fits — and when it doesn't.

To know you
is to understand your patterns,
your needs,
your limits,
your language.

And when you know yourself,
love stops being a chase.

It becomes recognition.

COMMENTARY

Love isn't discovered.
It's allowed.

SECTION 2 — Falling In Love With You First

Falling in love with yourself doesn't mean isolation.
It means alignment.

You stop auditioning.
You stop negotiating your nervous system.
You stop mistaking intensity for intimacy.

You learn what peace feels like —
and you stop apologizing for wanting it.

This isn't selfishness.
It's clarity.

COMMENTARY

You don't raise standards to exclude love.
You raise them to protect it.

SECTION 3 — How Love Meets You Differently Now

When you know yourself, love approaches differently.

It doesn't rush you.
It doesn't confuse you.
It doesn't demand you abandon yourself to be chosen.

Love meets you where you are —
because you finally stayed there.

And if it doesn't?
You don't force it.

You let it pass.

COMMENTARY

What's meant for you
won't require self-erasure.

SECTION 4 — What This Book Was Really About

This was never a book about leaving.

It was about **listening**.

Listening to your body.
Listening to patterns.
Listening to the moments you talked yourself out of truth.

It was about recognizing when love was real —
and when it was simply familiar.

And learning the difference
before it cost you more time.

COMMENTARY

Clarity doesn't make life easier.
It makes it honest.

FINAL WORDS — Big Sis Wrap-Up

Here's what Big Sis wants you to carry forward:

You are not behind.
You are not broken.
You were learning.

Every chapter you survived taught you something
about what you need,
what you deserve,
and what you will no longer tolerate.

Love doesn't ask you to disappear.
It doesn't need urgency.
It doesn't require endurance as proof.

To know you
is to respect you.
To love you
is to meet you without conditions.
And to fall in love with you
is the foundation everything else rests on.

Besides...
The real glow-up isn't who you attract next.
It's who you no longer abandon to keep someone.

And that —
is how this story ends.

BIG SIS' FINAL WORD — BEFORE YOU RISE

You didn't find this book by accident.
But you also didn't come here to be rescued.

You came because something in you was already awake —
questioning patterns,
noticing costs,
and getting tired of pretending you didn't see what you saw.

These pages weren't meant to reopen wounds.
They were meant to name them.

Because once something has language,
it stops owning you.

So before you move forward, pause here — just long enough to be
honest.

What did you recognize?
What did it cost you to survive it?
And what are you no longer willing to carry now that you see it clearly?

Your pain was real.
But it was never your identity.

It was information.

And clarity doesn't exist to shame your past —
it exists to change your future.

Healing isn't about understanding what happened.
That part is already done.

Healing is about what you *do differently* now that you know.

That's why this doesn't end with insight alone.

Insight needs practice.
Awareness needs repetition.
And growth needs a place to land.

The **Big Sis Self-Rescue Journal** isn't a requirement —
it's a resource.

Not homework.
Not performance.
Not perfection.

Just twelve weeks of checking in with yourself honestly.
Noticing patterns without judgment.
Choosing yourself consistently — not loudly, not flawlessly — but deliberately.

And hear this clearly:

The woman closing this book
is not the woman who opened it.

She doesn't rush anymore.
She doesn't confuse intensity with intimacy.
She doesn't override herself for love.

She pauses.
She listens.
She chooses.

Big Sis isn't proud of you for being healed.

She's proud of you for being honest enough to stop pretending.

So take a breath.
Take your clarity with you.
Take your power — it's yours now.

And when you're ready…

Rise.

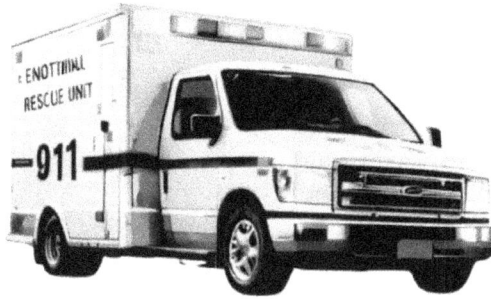

Big Sis Says

YOUR GLOW-UP IS
NOT REVENGE –
IT'S RECOVERY.
SHINE BECAUSE YOU
HEALED,
NOT BECAUSE THEY
WATCHED.

Speaking In Volumes Publishing creates transformational work centered on healing, identity restoration, and emotional clarity.

This work is rooted in lived experience, thoughtful reflection, and a grounded, conversational approach known as **Big Sis**— a voice that prioritizes truth without judgment and insight without overwhelm.

Alongside books and written work, **Life Be Lifing** offers optional programs, guided experiences, and small-group spaces designed to support continued reflection, boundary rebuilding, and personal clarity — at your own pace, in your own way.

We do not diagnose.
We do not shame.
We do not rush the process.

We support people in recognizing what happened, understanding how it shaped them, and reconnecting with themselves — without pressure to perform healing or reach conclusions.

For those who wish to continue the work:
www.lifebelifing.shop
Big Sis reflections: www.bigsis.life

www.ingramcontent.com/pod-product-compliance
Lightning Source LLC
Chambersburg PA
CBHW022049020426
42335CB00012B/603